Fruits Therapy

First Edition

Seyyed Mehdi Alemzadeh

Vancouver, BC CANADA

Copyright © 2024 by Kashti Nooh Publishing Inst.

All rights reserved. No part of this publication may be reproduced, distributed or transmitted in any form or by any means, including photocopying, recording, or other electronic or mechanical methods, without the prior written permission of the publisher, except in the case of brief quotations embodied in critical reviews and certain other noncommercial uses permitted by copyright law. For permission requests, write to the publisher, addressed "Attention: Permissions Coordinator," at the address below.

Published by: Kashti Nooh Publishing Inst.

Vancouver, BC **CANADA**
Email: Info@kashtinooh.com
www.kashtinooh.com

Ordering Information:
Quantity sales. Special discounts are available on quantity purchases by universities, schools, corporations, associations, and others. For details, contact the "Sales Department" at the above mentioned email address.

Fruits Therapy/S.M.Alemzadeh—1st. ed.
ISBN: 978-1-77899-006-9   Paperback

Every possible effort has been made to ensure that the information contained in this book is accurate at the time of going to press, and the publishers and the author cannot accept responsibility for any errors or omissions, however caused. No responsibility for loss or damage occasioned to any person acting, or refraining from action, as a result of the material in this publication can be accepted by the publisher and/or the author.

Fruits Therapy

Contents

1. Apple 1
   Other names: 1
   Latin name: 1
   Scientific name: 1
   Family: 1
   Medicinal forms: 1
   Medicinal Properties and usage: 2
   Ingredients: 6
   Specification: 7
2. Apricot 9
   Other names: 9
   Latin name: 9
   Scientific Name: 9
   Family: 9
   Medicinal Parts: 9
   Properties and Usage: 9
   Ingredients: 12
   Description: 13
3. Avocado 15
   Latin name: 15

Scientific name: 15
Medicinal properties: 15
Therapeutic Properties and Usage: 15
Composition: 15
Specifications: 16

4. Banana 17
Other names: 17
Scientific Name: 17
Medicinal forms: 17
Therapeutic properties and usage: 17
    Important note: 19
    Ingredients: 21
    Description: 22

5. Bergamot 25
Name: 25
Scientific Name: 25
Medicinal Forms: 25
Therapeutic Properties and Usage: 25
Ingredients: 25
Description: 26

6. Black Mulberry 27
Other names: 27
Latin name: 27

iii

Scientific name: 27
Medicinal forms: 27
Therapeutic properties and method of administration: 27
Ingredients: 29
Specifications: 29

7. Blackberry (Raspberry) 31
Other names: 31
Latin name: 31
Scientific name: 31
Medicinal forms: 31
Therapeutic properties and uses: 31
Composition: 33
Specifications: 34

8. Blackcurrant 36
Other names: 36
Latin name: 36
Scientific Name: 36
Medicinal forms: 36
Therapeutic properties and usage: 36
Ingredients: 37
Description: 37

9. Cherry 39
Other names: 39

Local names: 39
Latin name: 39
Scientific name: 39
Medicinal forms: 39
Therapeutic properties and usage: 40
    Gum: 41
Composition: 41
Specifications: 42

10. Clustered Red Currants (Red Gooseberry) 44
Other names: 44
Latin names: 44
Scientific name: 44
Medicinal forms: 44
Therapeutic properties and usage: 44
Composition: 45
    Preparation of red currant juice: 45
    Preparation of red currant juice or regular syrup: 45
Specifications: 46
Ghoreh Ghāt 46

11. Coconut 48
Other names: 48
Latin name: 48
Scientific name: 48

Medicinal forms: 48
Therapeutic properties and usage: 48
Composition: 51
Specifications: 52

12. Cornelian Cherry 54

Other names: 54
Latin name: 54
Scientific name: 54
Medicinal Properties and usage: 54
Specifications: 55

13. Cornus 56

Other names: 56
Latin name: 56
Scientific name: 56
Medicinal forms: 56
Therapeutic properties and usage: 56
Ingredients: 56
Plant Specifications: 57

14. Cucumber 58

Other names: 58
Scientific name: 58
Family: 58
Medicinal forms: 58

Medicinal properties and usage: 58
Components: 60
Characteristics: 61
15. Date Palm 62
Scientific name: 62
Medicinal forms: 62
Therapeutic Properties and Usage: 62
Specifications: 64
16. Fig 67
Other names: 67
Latin name: 67
Scientific name: 67
Medicinal forms: 67
Therapeutic properties and usage: 67
Composition: 69
Specifications: 71
17. Grapefruit 73
Latin name: 73
Scientific name: 73
Medicinal properties: 73
Therapeutic properties and usage: 73
Ingredients: 74
Characteristics: 75

18. Grapes 76
Other names: 76
Latin name: 76
Scientific Name: 76
Medicinal parts: 76
Therapeutic properties and usage: 76
Ghoreh (unripe grape): 78
Vinegar: 79
    Traditional method of vinegar preparation: 80
Raisin: 84
Ingredients 85
    A grape cluster generally consists of the following parts: 85
    Other substances: 86
    In every 100 grams of edible part of raw grapes (grape berries), the following substances are present: 86
Specifications 88

19. Green Plum 90
Other names: 90
Scientific name: 90
Medicinal forms: 90
Therapeutic properties and usage: 90
Characteristics: 91

20. Guava 92

Other names: 92
Latin name: 92
Scientific name: 92
Medicinal parts: 92
Therapeutic properties and usage: 92
Composition: 93
Description: 94

21. Hawthorn **96**
Other Names: 96
Other Latin names: 96
Scientific name: 96
Medicinal Properties and Usage: 96
Composition: 97
Characteristics: 98

22. Kiwi **102**
Latin name: 102
Scientific name: 102
Medicinal forms: 102
Medicinal Properties and Usage: 102
Composition: 103
Specifications: 103

23. Mango **105**
Other Names: 105

ix

Latin Name: 105
Scientific name: 105
Family: 105
Medicinal Forms: 105
Therapeutic Properties and Usage: 106
Sweetness: 107
Composition: 109
Specifications: 110

24. Medlar 111
Other names: 111
Latin name: 111
Scientific name: 111
Medicinal properties: 111
Therapeutic Properties and Usage: 111
Composition: 112
Specifications: 112

25. Nectarine Fruit 113
Other names: 113
Latin names: 113
Scientific name: 113
Medicinal forms: 113
Therapeutic properties and usage: 113
Ingredients: 116

Composition: 116
Specifications: 117
26. Orange 118
Latin Name: 118
Scientific name: 118
Family: 118
Medicinal Forms: 118
Therapeutic Properties and Usage: 118
Composition: 119
Specifications: 121
27. Papaya 123
Other Names: 123
Scientific name: 123
Medicinal Properties and Usage: 123
Composition: 126
Specifications: 127
28. Paper Mulberry 129
Other Names: 129
Scientific Name: 129
Family: 129
Parts Used: 129
Medicinal Properties and Usage 129
Components: 130

Specifications: 130
29. Peach 131
Other names: 131
Latin Name: 131
Scientific name: 131
Medicinal Forms: 131
Medicinal Properties and Usage: 131
Ingredients: 134
30. Pear 138
Other names: 138
Latin name: 138
Scientific name: 138
Medicinal forms: 138
Therapeutic properties and usage: 138
Ingredients: 140
Characteristics: 141
    Pyrus: 142
31. Persian melon 145
Other Names: 145
Scientific Name: 145
Family: 145
Parts Used: 145
Medicinal Properties and Usage: 145

Components: 148

Specifications: 148

32. Persimmon 149

Latin name: 149

Scientific name: 149

Medicinal properties and usage: 149

Composition: 150

Specifications: 151

33. Pineapple 152

Latin name: 152

Scientific name: 152

Medicinal forms: 152

Therapeutic properties and usage: 152

Ingredients: 153

Specifications: 153

34. Plum 155

Other names: 155

Latin name: 155

Scientific Name: 155

Medicinal forms: 155

Therapeutic properties and usage: 156

Usage methods: 157

Composition: 158

Specifications: 158

35. Pomegranate **161**

    Other names: 161

    Latin name: 161

    Scientific name: 161

    Medicinal forms: 161

    Properties and usage: 161

    Specifications: 166

36. Pomelo **168**

    Other names: 168

    Scientific name: 168

    Medicinal forms: 168

    Medicinal properties and uses: 168

    Composition: 169

    Characteristics: 169

37. Quince **171**

    Names: 171

    Latin Name: 171

    Scientific Name: 171

    Medicinal Forms: 171

    Therapeutic Properties and Usage: 171

    Composition: 174

    Fruit Composition: 174

Description: 175
38. Rose Apple 177
    Other Names: 177
    Scientific Name: 177
    Parts Used: 177
    Medicinal Properties and Usage: 177
    Components: 178
    Specifications: 178
39. Sour Cherry 179
    Other names: 179
    Scientific name: 179
    Medicinal forms: 179
    Therapeutic properties and usage: 179
    Ingredients: 180
    Characteristics: 181
40. Sour Lemon 182
    Other names: 182
    Latin name: 182
    Scientific name: 182
    Medicinal forms: 182
    Therapeutic properties and usage: 182
    Composition: 184
    Specifications: 185

41. Strawberry 186
Other Names: 186
Latin Name: 186
Scientific name: 186
Family: 186
Medicinal forms: 186
Therapeutic properties and usage: 187
Ingredients: 187
Specifications: 188

42. Sweet Lemon 190
Latin name: 190
Scientific name: 190
Medicinal forms: 190
Medicinal properties and uses: 190
Composition: 191
Specifications: 191

43. Tangerine 192
Other names: 192
Latin Names: 192
Scientific Name: 192
Medicinal Forms: 192
Medicinal Properties and Usage: 193
Composition: 193

Specifications: 194

44. Thorny Gooseberry 195

Other names for gooseberry: 195

Latin names: 195

Scientific Name: 195

Medicinal forms: 195

Therapeutic properties and usage: 195

Composition: 196

Specifications: 196

45. Watermelon 197

Latin name: 197

Scientific Name: 197

Medicinal forms: 197

Therapeutic properties and method of Usage: 197

Components: 199

Specifications: 200

46. White Mulberry 201

Other names: 201

Latin name: 201

Scientific name: 201

Family: 201

Medicinal forms: 202

Therapeutic properties and usage 202

xvii

Components: 203
Specifications: 204
47. Wild Tomato (Solanum pimpinellifolium) 205
Other names: 205
Latin name: 205
Scientific name: 205
Medicinal properties and usage: 205
Composition: 206
Description: 206

1. Apple

Other names:

Tafah, Dham Hasib, Seif, Tarsh Hesi, Seh, Alma Siu, Su.

Latin name:

Apple.

Scientific name:

In Iranian botanical literature is Malus, European: orientalis, American: Malus communis, Indian: Malus pumila Mill.

Family:

Rosaceae.

Medicinal forms:

Fruit, leaf, root.

Medicinal Properties and usage:

From a nature perspective, sweet apples are warm and moist, while sour apples are cold, and dry. The tree's components are generally cold and dry. Both the leaves and the fruit have detoxifying properties. Apples are good for strengthening the brain and liver, aiding digestion, and stimulating appetite. Sweet apples are joyful and soothing to the spirit, and cooked apples are beneficial for dry coughs.

In India, eating apples is useful for preventing constipation and acts as a mild laxative. Apple tree bark decoction is used as an antipyretic and for the treatment of intermittent fevers, including malaria and bilious fevers. In China, apple roots are used as anthelmintics, cooling agents, and sleep aids. Other documents mention the apple tree bark as the main active ingredient. Apple tree leaves have diuretic properties, and the decoction of the leaves[1] is used to alleviate kidney and bladder inflammation.

Apple fruit has antidiarrheal, laxative, diuretic, and soothing properties, and it is recommended to consume it with the skin. Cooked apples act as a laxative and are useful for relieving insomnia. Apples also help prevent Uric acid formation and

---

1. To prepare apple leaf decoction, take 120 grams of apple leaves, and for apple tree bark decoction, take 120 grams of apple tree bark. Boil them in 1000 grams of water for about 15 minutes, then consume one or two cups.
Uric acid builds up in the body, and consuming it is beneficial for gout, rheumatism, and cold-related conditions.

eating it for sweet rheumatism gout has beneficial effects in cases of cold[1], hoarseness and cough.

Cooked apple fruit has a laxative, sleep-inducing, and soothing effect. To prepare a decoction, take 10 grams of dried apple peel and boil it in 100 grams of water for about 15 minutes, then consume.

The water of apple decoction, mixed with a little vinegar and meat broth, is effective for relieving indigestion. Steaming apples retains all their properties, and the raw fruit is stronger in its raw state. It is beneficial for calming the heart, strengthening the stomach and liver, relieving acidity, obsession, and eliminating toxins, especially scorpion venom. It provides relief from heat and also apple jam has the same properties.[2]

Eating boiled apple is highly beneficial for bloody diarrhea and beneficial for individuals suffering from tuberculosis, shortness of breath, and weight loss.

Applying a poultice of apple on the eyes is useful for relieving eye pain. Excessive consumption of unripe apples causes fever and creates discomforts such as bloating, cramps, muscle pain, and sudden body jerks. In such cases, it is recommended to use cinnamon and light foods.

---

1. An American article from 1927 states that apples are useful for treating various conditions that lead to acidosis in the body, as well as for gout, rheumatism, jaundice, and various liver and gallbladder disorders. It is also effective in relieving sourness and various internal intoxication conditions.
2. Refers to an apple that is taken in dough and cooked over fire until it is fully cooked.

Sour apples have astringent properties and alleviate thirst and dryness. They are useful for people with biliary stomachs, and cooked sour apples in dough are beneficial for bloody diarrhea. Sour apple juice mixed with pomegranate juice and appropriate medications is beneficial for strengthening the stomach and relieving biliary diarrhea and thirst. Excessive consumption of sour apples is harmful to the chest, and for its correction, one should use sugar cane, cinnamon, and honey. Sour and sweet apples produce beneficial and compatible humors and relieve thirst and biliary conditions.

Raw, unripe, tasteless apples are harmful and cause discomfort and fever.

Apple leaf poultice is useful for warm swellings at the beginning of the swelling, and apple blossom with suitable drugs is effective for removing the infected mixture, and apple blossom jam or in other words sugar flower from apple flowers is useful for weakness of the heart and nose and to stimulate sexual power. For this purpose, apple blossom is mixed with twice its weight of rose flower juice and eaten. It is recommended that hot-tempered people always eat sour apples or sweet and sour apples and cold-tempered people should eat sweet apples, although sweet apples are not harmful for hot-tempered people either.

Recommendations: The more apples are consumed naturally and completely, the more likely it is for blood cholesterol levels to decrease in proportion to individuals. It seems for unknown reasons that after eating an apple, women's blood cholesterol decreases more than men's.

In the first three weeks of consuming a large amount of apples, total cholesterol may slightly increase, but it gradually decreases afterward and becomes lower than the normal level. However, French studies have shown that the cholesterol-lowering effect of apples is not universal for all individuals. It is always recommended to eat apples with their skin, provided that the stomach condition allows it, and they should be chewed well. Sweet, ripe, and fresh apples have a high content of pectin in their skin. However, apple juice contains a very small amount of pectin to the extent that it cannot be expected to reduce cholesterol and blood pressure or balance blood sugar. Additionally, the chemical substances with anti-cancer properties in apple water are very low.

Caution: Apple cider or clarified apple juice suppresses the natural ability to dissolve blood clots, so it should be avoided as consuming it makes the blood vulnerable and increases the likelihood of clot formation. However, natural apple extract does not have such negative effects. Even a small amount of apple extract may worsen chronic diarrhea in some children, according to researchers.

The vitamins in apples are mostly found in the apple skin, so it is more beneficial to consume apples with the skin. In remote areas, dried or fresh apple leaf buds are added to boiling water, which makes it refreshing. Consuming ripe and juicy apples is beneficial for acute intestinal disorders, bloody diarrhea, certain types of fevers, and similar conditions in children. Dried apple skin, when brewed, is very useful for reducing joint swelling, rheumatism, gout, and kidney discomfort that leads to decreased urine production, as it acts as a diuretic and helps regulate the digestive system, facilitating the elimination of uric acid. Consuming 50 grams of apple syrup is very pleasant, refreshing, disinfecting, and cooling.[1]

Ingredients:

In apple leaves, about 1% of florizin glucosides are present, and in its seeds, in addition to amygdalin, about 8% of its fresh weight consists of florizin glucosides. Another study shows that apple leaves contain a bactericidal substance called floritin, which is about 2.4% and prevents the growth of a large number of Gram-positive and Gram-negative bacteria when their density is low, around 30 ppm. Ripe apples contain a considerable amount of hydrated carbon compounds, of which about 80% are various sugars. These sugars consist of approximately 60% fructose, 25% glucose, and 15% sucrose. In the edible part of the apple, about 0.96-0.14% pectin is present in the form of calcium.

If they take about 200 grams of the root of the mulberry tree and create a crack in it, along with 30 grams of hair leaf and 30 grams of black fig, and pour some water into a container, closing its lid

---

1. Researchers at Konk Tech University have reported that a few of their sick children, aged 31-13 months, showed a reaction and developed symptoms of diarrhea after consuming apple water. They believe that some children may not be able to absorb apple sugars completely. 1. However, for individuals whose stomach condition allows them to eat raw apple skin... 2. To prepare apple syrup, finely chop 2-3 ripe apples, boil them in a sufficient amount of water to obtain a total of 1000 grams, strain the mixture, add sugar to it, and prepare the apple syrup.

tightly, and boil it until it reaches one-sixth, it will result in a beautiful and good hair dye. Similarly, the infusion of mulberry leaf or hair leaf and black fig has the same effect. Consuming about 30 grams of leaf extract is beneficial for picking animals and sting insects. Also, the boiled skin of the mulberry tree is a shocker poison. For this purpose, the skin should be boiled in water. Usually, after eating sour food, especially after mulberries, it is not advisable to eat mulberries because mulberry leaves contain a considerable amount of calcium carbonate, so the infusion of mulberry leaves can be used to reduce urinary sugar and treat diabetes.

The following ingredients are found in each hundred grams of the edible part of raw apple fruit; Water, about 85 grams of carbohydrates, 5.13 grams of calcium, 7 mg of iron, 3 mg of carbohydrates, 3 mg of sodium, 1 mg of potassium, 110 mg of vitamin A, about 90 international units of thiamin, 03 mg of riboflavin. Flavin, 02 mg of niacin, 1 mg of vitamin C and mg of phosphorus.

Specification:

Apple is a tree with a medium height and its bark is gray and its leaves are simple, elongated oval, on hairy leaves, measuring about 3.5-8 x 1.5-3 cm. Its flowers are large with a diameter of 4-5 cm, the color of the flowers is white and their back is pink. Its fruit is round, its domestic and cultivated varieties are large, juicy, and its wild varieties are small, and its taste is sweet in some cultivars, sour in some cultivars, and sour and sweet in some cultivars. Domestic apples are planted in most regions of the world, especially in mountainous and temperate regions. In Iran, it grows wildly in the forests of the north of Iran at different altitudes from the Jalga to the upper parts of the forest, even in the steppe areas. It also grows in the southern slopes of Alborz, and in addition, it grows in Arjan Plain, Niriz, Shahpur Fort in Kurdistan, in Bakhtran, Harsin Biston, and in Lorestan, in Darud. Its wild types are seen.

Its domesticated and cultivated varieties are also planted in most regions of Iran. Apple propagation is done by grafting the cultivated cultivars on wild apple bases. Usually, abdominal grafting is done in summer at a distance of 68 cm from the soil.

2. Apricot

Other names:
Shakarpareh, Qaisi Mashmash, Khoobani (leaves).

Latin name:
Aotucit tree.

Scientific Name:
Prunus armeniaca.

Family:
Rosaceae.

Medicinal Parts:
Fruit, kernel, leaves, flowers.

Properties and Usage:

Apricot is considered cool and moist in nature, and its sweetness is slightly warm. It has properties that help open clogged vessels and soften hardness. Sweet apricot is a mild laxative and beneficial for individuals with warm temperaments. It also helps alleviate bad breath. In traditional medicine, the kernel of the apricot is used for treating chest ailments, dryness of the throat and pharynx, as well as for diseases of the lungs and edema. In China and Japan, it is used as a blood purifier, cough suppressant, respiratory tonic, anticonvulsant, and for severe colds, bronchial asthma, rheumatism, leg edema, and constipation. Boiling mature apricot leaves can stimulate appetite. The oil extracted from its kernel is added to cough medicines.

In India and China, it is common to chew soaked or boiled apricot pits without swallowing them. It is believed that the bronchial tubes are protected from the cold during winter, thus avoiding damage. Some believe that the flower, leaves, kernel, and all aerial parts of the plant are effective in the mentioned conditions.

Drinking boiled or soaked apricot leaves acts as a cholagogue and mild laxative. It relieves thirst, reduces blood and bile fever, and alleviates stomach inflammation. If a person with a fever caused by warm bile eats apricots and drinks warm water with honey on it, their fever will subside. Apricots spoil quickly and can become rotten; they are flatulent and can cause sour belching in such cases, and may even cause fever. It is harmful for individuals with cold temperaments and weak stomachs, especially elderly individuals. To avoid these harms, it is recommended to consume apricots with sugar, vinegar, anise, cumin, or cardamom. If water is consumed with apricots, especially if the water is cold or if apricots are eaten after a heavy meal, it can be very harmful.

In order to correct it, they should try and make enemas with Helilah or fennel seeds for several days in a row, or by eating saffron. It is very bad to eat apricots on an empty stomach, and if you continue to eat them, it will cause heartache, and to cure it, you should eat sugar and anise. If the apricot kernel is bitter, it is hot and dry, and if it is sweet, it is less hot and dry, and in terms of sexual power tonic properties and slow digestion, it should be roasted and eaten with salt. open the kernel oil, both bitter and sweet; It is spasms and removes the harshness of the throat and roughness of the skin. Eating 5 grams of its bitter nut oil kills stomach worms and is a strong laxative, dissolves swelling of the anus, and crushes bladder stones. Pouring a few drops of it in the ear is useful to relieve ear pain and remove the heaviness of hearing, and in other properties it is very similar to bitter almond oil.

Its feed amount is up to 15 grams and its sweet nut oil is weaker than its bitter one. Eating the bitter pith of the apricot kernel may cause poisoning and confusion, and the remedy is to vomit it, and it is resolved by eating sour fruit pastes. Apricot leaves and blossoms are cold and dry by nature, and eating a decoction of its leaves repels stomach worms and diuretics, and pouring it on swellings causes the swellings to dissolve. If 10 grams of its dry leaves are eaten with cold water, it stops and stops diarrhea, and if a few drops of its juice are poured into the ear, it relieves ear pain. Eating apricot blossoms has the same properties as its leaves. Dried apricot blossoms stop internal and external bleeding.

Ingredients:

The presence of fatty oil and ethereal oil, several enzymes and amygdalin have been reported in apricot kernels, and lycopene, alpha-carotene and vitamin A are found in apricot fruit. In another report, it is stated that there are fatty oil and proin, arabinose sugar, essential oil ash, volatile, amygdalozide, emulsin, lactase, cellobase and vitamins C and A in the kernel of the apricot kernel. Amygdalin glucoside is converted to glucose, sciatic acid and benzaldehyde under the influence of enzymes and water. It decomposes into Chiu) and Karione and Kimura. Cyanic acid is a toxic compound with the formula HOCN.

Each one hundred grams of sweet apricot meat contains the following ingredients:

Water: 85 grams.

Carbohydrates: 12 grams.

Protein: 1 gram.

Ash: 0.7 grams.

Calcium: 0.7 milligrams.

Phosphorus: 23 milligrams.

Iron: 0.5 milligrams.

Sodium: 1 milligram.

Potassium: 281 milligrams.

Vitamin A: 2700 international units.

Thiamine: 0.03 milligrams.

Riboflavin: 0.04 milligrams.

Niacin: 0.6 milligrams.

Magnesium: significant amount.

Description:

The Apricot tree is a deciduous tree that reaches a height of 4-6 meters with a spherical crown. Its trunk is greenish-brown in color when young and develops noticeable cracks in mature trees, turning reddish. The leaves are simple, heart-shaped, shiny green with serrated edges and a long petiole. The flowers appear in early spring and are white or pink, without a tail, appearing singly or in pairs. The fruit, found in both wild and cultivated varieties, is relatively large, sweet, round, slightly egg-shaped, and has yellowish flesh. It contains a hard woody pit, which is smoother than that of a peach and usually does not stick to the flesh in most varieties. Inside the pit, there is a kernel similar to an almond with a thin skin, which can taste sweet or bitter. The

Apricot fruit is usually harvested in July and August in moderate climates.

The Apricot is native to Manchuria, Mongolia, and northern China, and it was initially believed to be native to Armenia, which is why it is named after Armenia. In Iran, it is cultivated in steppe regions and has various cultivars.

Apricot propagation is done through grafting, and the Apricot pit is only used to obtain rootstock for grafting. The most commonly used grafting methods for plums are side-veneer grafting and using rootstocks obtained from Apricot pits. In areas with deep soil and warm, sunny climates, rootstocks obtained from Apricot pits are usually used. In areas with calcareous soil, almond is used as the rootstock for Apricot. In some regions, wild almond is chosen as the rootstock for grafting Apricot, but unfortunately, it often produces non-grafted shoots. Apricot grafting is typically done at a height of 810 centimeters above the ground.

3. Avocado

Latin name:

Avocadopear and Avocado.

Scientific name:

Persea americana Mill from the family Lauraceae.

Medicinal properties:

Fruit, leaves, and seeds.

Therapeutic Properties and Usage:

Avocado strengthens the stomach. In the Philippines, boiled avocado leaves are eaten to relieve back pain and stop bloody diarrhea. Its seeds are also used as medicine. In industry, avocado oil is used to add fragrance to various creams. The fruit contains various essential fatty acids and vitamins and is very nutritious, delicious, and useful when used as a sauce in salads.

Composition:

The flesh of the fruit is fatty, and a solid oil is extracted from its seeds that contain about seven percent saturated fatty acids such as palmitic acid, stearic acid, arachidic acid, myristic acid, and about 80 percent unsaturated fatty acids such as oleic acid, linoleic acid, etc. This oil quickly turns rancid when exposed to air. In every 100 grams of edible and consumable avocado fruit, the following substances are present: water 74 grams, protein 2 grams, fat 16 grams, carbohydrates 6 grams, ash 2.1 grams, calcium 10 milligrams, phosphorus 42 milligrams, iron 6.0 milligrams, sodium 4 milligrams, potassium 604 milligrams, vitamin A 290 international units, thiamine 11.0 milligrams, riboflavin 20.0 milligrams, niacin 6.1 milligrams, and vitamin C 14 milligrams.

Specifications:

Avocado is a small shrub that is used for consumption and medicinal purposes. Its fruit is pear-shaped and has a brownish-purple exterior but a greenish interior flesh. The nut inside the fruit is round with two lips. This plant is grown in Brazil, warm parts of America, western India, and some other parts of the world.

4. Banana

Other names:

Talah, Latin names: Banana and Plantain.

Scientific Name:

Musa sapientum, from the Musaceae family.

Medicinal forms:

Fruit, flower, round, root, syrup.

Therapeutic properties and usage:

From a nature perspective, banana is considered moderately warm and moist. In terms of its properties, it is believed to be slow to digest and can create thick blood and promote weight gain. It softens the chest and is beneficial when applied to baldness, scabies, and itching when mixed with vinegar and lemon juice. Banana flesh is useful for dry coughs, throat irritation, and stomach moistening, and stimulating sexual potency in individuals with warm temperaments. Banana leaf poultices are beneficial for relieving swelling, wounds, and burns.

However, excessive consumption of bananas can cause the production of gas, bloating, and thick phlegmatic blood. It can worsen digestive weakness, especially in individuals with cold temperaments and those with a moist temperament, particularly if the banana is soaked in water. To alleviate these symptoms, it is recommended to consume salt after eating bananas. In individuals with cold temperaments, after eating bananas, consuming ginger preserves, honey, and sugar is advised, while in individuals with warm temperaments experiencing such symptoms, they should consume skunkvine. Eating bananas on an empty stomach is harmful in general. Bananas are generally beneficial for individuals with warm temperaments and dryness, especially in warm regions. However, they are detrimental and can cause adverse effects in individuals with cold temperaments, weakness, and humid areas. Banana roots are warm and dry, and consuming them helps expel intestinal worms. Applying banana peel ash to wounds is useful for stopping bleeding and promoting wound healing.[1]

---

1. It is recommended to always use unripe green bananas. Unripe green bananas contain the most potent nutritional substances, and usually, the larger and thicker the banana, the greater its therapeutic effects. Researchers believe that ripe bananas have fewer active therapeutic chemicals. In South America, India, and Africa, unripe bananas are boiled or roasted and eaten, similar to potatoes. All types of bananas have similar medicinal properties to some extent.

Important note:

In traditional Indian medicine, unripe bananas are considered astringent in addition to two active substances: serotonin and norepinephrine. Bananas also contain dopamine and an unspecified catecholamine. The concentration and amount of these substances differ in the peel and flesh of the banana. The medicinal properties of bananas in treating constipation, peptic ulcers, and other conditions are attributed to these active substances.[1]

Banana has a mild laxative effect and is beneficial for simple constipation and bloody diarrhea. It accelerates the healing of intestinal ulcers. Banana flower is useful in treating hemorrhoids and relieving intestinal irregularities. Unripe fruits and cooked flowers of the banana are beneficial for diabetes. Banana flower syrup is used for bloody diarrhea, and its stem and root are useful for blood disorders.[2]

Banana root and the ash of the whole plant have anthelmintic properties. The unripe fruit, along with other medications, is used to treat diabetes. In China, the root, juice, fruit, and flower of the banana have medicinal uses. Shredded banana root is applied to various severe wounds, carbuncles, tumors, sunburns, and headaches with fever. The syrup obtained from shredded banana

---

1. Incompletely ripened green bananas are believed to contain the best type of beneficial plant fibers for the heart. It is characterized by chronic illness with symptoms such as mouth ulcers, indigestion, diarrhea, weight loss, and anemia.
2. To obtain plant sap, a hole is made in the banana stem and a spigot is inserted inside it, allowing the sap to be extracted.

root is used for treating jaundice, reducing thirst, alleviating scabies, toothaches, and syphilis-related fevers. The syrup obtained from the stem of the plant is also beneficial for headaches accompanied by fever and is used for strengthening hair. Dry banana leaf powder mixed with sesame oil or fresh ginger syrup is beneficial for dissolving and reducing swelling and abscesses. If applied at the initial stages of boils, scabies, and abscesses, it helps in their resolution. Banana Fruit, when dried and powdered, strengthens the body and is consumed as a tonic.

Dry banana leaf powder mixed with sesame oil or fresh ginger syrup is beneficial for dissolving and reducing swelling and abscesses. If applied at the initial stages of boils, scabies, and abscesses, it helps in their resolution. Banana fruit, when dried and powdered, strengthens the body and is consumed as a tonic.

Bananas represent 159 calories. Some people mix a small amount of its pollen with salt and water to consume it as a heart tonic and for relieving pain accompanied by fever. In India and China, the terminal buds of the branches are given to breastfeeding mothers to increase their milk secretion. Bananas are beneficial for stomach discomfort and chronic diarrhea. In Indonesia, the boiled fruit is used to stop bleeding, and the boiled roots are used for the same purpose as a hot bath to treat stomach cancer in Africa. In Brazil, young banana leaves are used to treat nasal cancer and tumors. The leaves are boiled with almond oil, and the warm mixture is applied. Banana fruit is useful for treating cancerous ulcers.

Ingredients:

Bananas contain two potent chemical compounds: serotin, which stimulates the smooth muscles of the intestines, and norepinephrine, which is used to treat certain types of heart diseases.

The banana peel contains approximately 14.7% dry matter and 1.6% invert sugar.

In every 100 grams of banana flesh, the following substances are present:[1]

Water: 74%.

Sugar: 8.5%.

Cellulose: 4.2%.

Non-crystalline sugar: 6.4%.

Starch: 3.3%.

Fats: 0.30%.

Organic acids and tannins: 4.2%.

Pectin: 0.2%.

Nitrogenous substances: 0.6%.

Minerals: 1.1%.

---

1. Invert sugar refers to non-crystallizable sugar formed due to the action of invertin.

In terms of minerals, vitamins, and other substances, the following are present in every 100 grams of raw banana flesh:

Water: 74 grams.

Sugars and other carbon hydrates: as mentioned above.

Calcium: 8 mg.

Phosphorus: 26 mg.

Iron: 0.7 mg.

Sodium: 1 mg.

Potassium: 370 mg.

Vitamin A: 190 international units.

Thiamine: 0.05 mg.

Riboflavin: 0.06 mg.

Niacin: 0.7 mg.

Vitamin C: 10 mg.

Description:

The banana plant is a large perennial herbaceous plant that resembles a small tree, but its stems are herbaceous. Its leaves are large, several centimeters long, with their lower parts rolled into tubes and twisted together to form a thick stem, which is actually the lower extension of the twisted leaves. The width of the leaves is about 50-30 centimeters, they are light green, and they collectively form a canopy at the top of the plant's trunk, while the inflorescence of the plant appears between the leaves. Its fruit comes in the form of a dense cluster consisting of dozens of bananas. Its fruiting pattern is such that after each fruiting, the leaves and stems wither away, and another stem composed of leaves emerges from the underground part of the plant, which also gives way to another stem after bearing fruit.

Among the various edible bananas, three types are notable:

1. Bananaier des sages or Musa sapientum, known as Sweet plantain in English. Its fruit is small, highly fragrant, very delicious, and sweet.
2. Bananir de paradis or Musa paradisiaca, commonly referred to as plantain, its fruit is starchy and is usually consumed after cooking.
3. Musa sinensis, also known as Chinese banana, is cultivated in most parts of the world as a high-quality banana; it is fragrant, sweet, and highly favored.

Banana propagation is done through suckers that emerge from its roots. Once these suckers reach a height of 80 centimeters, they are separated and planted at a distance of 2-3 meters from the mother plant. The banana is native to tropical regions and is also cultivated in the southern parts of Iran. The fruit is cylindrical, elongated, and depending on the type of banana, it has a diameter of 12-3 centimeters and a length of 30-5 centimeters. The skin of the fruit is usually greenish-yellow and turns slightly brown after ripening and staying for a while. The inner part of the fruit has sweet white flesh, and in some varieties, it is highly aromatic and delicious. The banana fruit usually does not develop seeds. The skin accounts for about 40% of the banana, while the flesh makes up 60%.

5. Bergamot

Name:

Bergamot orange of Europe or Bergamot.

Scientific Name:

Citrus bergamia Risso et Poit, from the Rutaceae family.

Medicinal Forms:

Fruit, Leaves.

Therapeutic Properties and Usage:

Bergamot leaves are anthelmintic, vermifuge, and stomach tonic. Its ripe fruit is appetizing and aids digestion, while its ripe fruit acts as a sexual stimulant. Bergamot essential oil is an antiseptic and is used in the cosmetics industry.

Ingredients:

The peel of bergamot contains essential oils such as linalyl acetate, limonene, linalool, and terpinene.

Other studies indicate that bergamot essential oil contains approximately 50% limonene and 40% linalool.

Description:

It is a type of citrus plant that is a small tree, about 4 meters tall, and is actually an orange without thorns. Its leaves are similar to orange leaves with hairy petioles. Its flowers resemble white and fragrant oranges. Its fruit resembles a pear with yellow, smooth, shiny, light yellow skin, and has a slightly sour taste.

6. Black Mulberry

Other names:
Shami mulberry, Black mulberry.

Latin name:
Black mulberry.

Scientific name:
Morus nigra L from the family Moraceae.

Medicinal forms:
Fruit, root, leaf.

Therapeutic properties and method of administration:

It is cold and dry in nature, and dry black mulberry is a substitute for sumac in terms of properties. It softens and loosens spasms, relieves the severity of blood and eliminates the effects of bile, and relieves swelling of the pharynx and larynx. It quenches thirst and awakens appetite.Gargling with its juice or paste is useful for bad wounds, mouth ulcers, analysis of swelling of the pharynx, palate and tongue and strengthening them, especially if it is mixed with fresh coriander leaf juice or chicory leaf juice, or with marmaki, or saffron, or Irsa, or frankincense. .Eating blackberries is very useful for intestinal ulcers and warm diarrhea and especially dry bloody diarrhea with auxiliary and tonic drugs. Blackberries are harmful to the chest, lungs, and nerves, and in this regard, they should be eaten with honey and sweet pomegranate juice.

Black mulberry paste is the vicegerent of its fruit. Mulberry and black mulberry root brew, which is brewed with about 40 grams of root, is useful for expelling worms, especially if peach leaves are added to it. If half-pounded black mulberry root is boiled in 40 grams per half kilogram of water until it reaches a quarter and sugar and honey are poured into it, it is very beneficial to remove toxins and insanity and back and back pain caused by raw phlegm. Eating a decoction of its leaves also has the same effect, and gargling it is beneficial for Scrofula[1]. Eating a brew of 30 grams of its root stems with 100 grams of figs that have been boiled in half a kilogram of water and reduced to half is a strong purgative of soda.

If the juice of black mulberry root, which has been taken by making a crack in it, about 200 grams with 30 grams of hair leaves and 30 grams of black figs and a little water in a container, close the lid tightly and boil until it reaches one-sixth and remove

---

1. Hard glands that are found in the neck and under the throat and sometimes turn into wounds and pus comes out of them; Tuberculosis and lymph nodes.

the hair. It is beautiful and good to wash with it. Also, the infusion of black mulberry leaves or hair leaves and black figs has the same result. Eating its leaf extract in about 30 grams is useful for biting animals and biting insects. Also, the decoction of black mulberry tree bark is hemlock poison. For this, the bark should be boiled in water. Usually, sour food should not be eaten after eating berries, especially after blackberries. Because there is a considerable amount of calcium carbonate in black mulberry leaves, its brew can be used to reduce urine sugar and treat diabetes.

Ingredients:

In the juice of unripe mulberry fruit, there is about 2-3% citric acid. In ripe fruit, it contains about 12% sugar and in some very sweet varieties, up to 20% sugar, along with a small amount of gum, a partial amount of malic acid, and a considerable amount of fat.

Specifications:

The mulberry tree[1] is a tree that is shorter than white mulberry and reaches about 10-15 meters in height. Its trunk is gray, its

---

1. The mulberry tree is usually short, with a height of 4-5 meters, and sometimes it reaches up to 20 meters. Its leaves are heart-shaped with a long leaf stalk, and its flowers are separate male and female flowers, each on a male base and a female base. Some mulberry trees have only male bases, which do not bear fruit, while others have aborted female bases and bear

leaves are dark green and rough with a completely heart-shaped base and a short leaf stalk. Its fruits are large, wrinkled, and turn into a dark plum-like color when ripe, and they have a sour taste. In Iran, it is usually called "Shah Tut" in Yazd, "Tut-e-Siyah" (black mulberry) in Hamadan.

Mulberry is native to Iran and Asia Minor. In Iran, it is seen in a wild state in West Azerbaijan and around the Qasemloo Valley. It is also seen in the heights of Kermanshah in the foothills of Mount Paro and in the highlands of Birjand.

---

fruit. There are also varieties of mulberry trees that have both male and female bases on one tree.

7. Blackberry (Raspberry)

Other names:

Giheh Koohi, Aliq (Aliq al-Jabal), Tut-e Shuki, Tomosh, Lem, Walash-Lush, Handal, Tuzak Darduk, Todz.

Latin name:

Blackberry and Brambie.

Scientific name:

Rubus saxatilis L belongs to the Rosaceae family, genus Rubus.

Medicinal forms:

Fruit, leaf, stem.

Therapeutic properties and uses:

In terms of nature, it is considered balanced, but it tends towards coldness and dryness. It is believed that all parts of the plant have cooling and drying properties. It stops bleeding, stops chest bleeding, and stops uterine bleeding. It strengthens the intestines and internal organs. Applying its leaf as a dressing is beneficial for healing head wounds and eye inflammation. In India, the decoction of the root of the species R.fruticosus is consumed to treat diarrhea with blood and is very beneficial for severe cough attacks and alleviating black cough.

The decoction of the plant's leaves is used to treat diarrhea and stop certain bleeding. The plant is generally beneficial for strengthening the heart and is also a laxative. In China, blackberries are generally consumed as tonics to enhance sexual strength and vitality. The fresh green leaves and stems, mixed with a little gum arabic, are beneficial for hot head and eye diseases, especially for eye ulcers, tearing, and swelling. Chewing the leaf or fruit is beneficial for gum wounds, gum weakness, mouth odor, and fresh mouth surgeries. Drinking the juice of fresh green leaves and stems, mixed with a little gum arabic, is beneficial for stomach strengthening and prevention of diarrhea and bleeding from the chest.

Applying a bandage of its leaf or a concentrated extract of its leaf, shaded in a thick shade, is beneficial for preventing hemorrhoids bleeding. Its fruit is more astringent than other parts, and eating it is beneficial for strengthening the gums. The species R.saxatilis is used as a substitute for R.fruticosus in terms of medicinal properties.

Hot head and eye diseases include eye congestion, visual weakness due to heat, eye pain, and some dizziness.

The intestines and consuming the root bark of mulberry are beneficial for crushing kidney stones. Applying mulberry leaf poultice helps analyze and prevent swelling, as well as applying fresh mulberry fruit juice or flower extract to dry wounds and prevent pus flow. Steeping mulberry leaves and fruit can be used as a natural hair dye. Mulberry is harmful to the kidneys and should be consumed with caution when sweetened. The recommended dosage of its flower extract is 12-14 grams.

Composition:

Lactic acid, succinic acid, malic acid, oxalic acid, tannins, and confirmed albuminoids have been found in the leaves of the fruticosus species of mulberry. Cyanidin-monoglucoside is found in mulberry fruits.

Per 100 grams of edible part of various mulberry types, the average composition is as follows: water 84.5 grams, protein 1.2 grams, fat 0.9 grams, carbohydrates 9 grams, ash 0.5 grams, calcium 32 milligrams, phosphorus 19 milligrams, iron 0.9 milligrams, sodium 1 milligram, potassium 170 milligrams, vitamin A 200 international units, thiamine 0.03 milligrams, riboflavin 0.04 milligrams, niacin 0.4 milligrams, and vitamin C 21 milligrams.

Per 100 grams of raw scented mulberry fruit, the following substances are present: black mulberry water 80 grams, protein 1.5 grams, fat 1.4 grams, carbohydrates 15 grams, calcium 30 milligrams, phosphorus 22 milligrams, iron 0.9 milligrams, sodium 1 milligram, potassium 199 milligrams, vitamin A (partial) 0.30 milligrams, riboflavin 0.09 milligrams, niacin 0.9 milligrams, and vitamin C 18 milligrams.

Per 100 grams of red mulberry, the following substances are present: water 84 grams, protein 1.2 grams, fat 0.5 grams, carbohydrates 13 grams, calcium 22 milligrams, phosphorus 22 milligrams, iron 0.9 milligrams, sodium 1 milligram, potassium 168 milligrams, vitamin A 130 international units, thiamine 0.03 milligrams, riboflavin 0.09 milligrams, niacin 0.9 milligrams, and vitamin C 25 milligrams.

Specifications:

Mulberry is a plant with various species that grow in different regions of the world. Mulberries have two major types: one produces a single crop, and the other produces two crops. The latter is known as Remontantes, yielding one crop in spring and another in autumn.

The scientific name and medicinal properties of several species have been examined and are of interest. They include:

Rubus saxatilis L.:[1] A perennial plant with short, simple branches covered with fine hairs and sharp thorns. The leaves are green

---

1. Domesticated raspberry species are referred to as "Giaha" and "Domestic Raspberry" in Persian and are commonly grown in gardens. They also belong to the Rosaceae family. In general, they are called "Raspberry" in English. Their fruit is sweet and aromatic and comes in various colors such as red, black, and purple. The well-known scientific names of some species are as follows: 1) Red Raspberry, known as Rubus idaeus in Latin. 2) Black Raspberry, known as Rubus occidentalis in Latin. 3) Purple Raspberry, known as Rubus ursinus in Latin.

and covered with tiny hairs. The flowers, appearing at the end of flowering branches, are pink in color and occur naturally in Lahijan, Iran, and the Tibetan region of Kashmir to Taku Maun in India.

Aubus Caesius L: Commonly known as "blueberry" and found in various regions of northern and northwest Iran, as well as the surrounding areas of Tehran, Alborz, and Eshtehranakouh. The local name for this plant in Alborz and Eshtehranakouh is "Tudar."

This perennial plant has cylindrical stems with multiple branches covered in slender, thorny prickles. The green leaves are almost without petioles and consist of five egg-shaped leaflets, some of which have glands, while others do not. The leaves have fine hairs on the upper surface and a white felt-like covering on the lower surface. The white flowers and the fruit, resembling blackberries, are dark blue in color.

Rubus fruticosus, also known as Common blackberry or Common bramble, is a perennial plant that uses its strong and numerous thorns on stems and branches to climb and attach itself to neighboring plants. The flowers are white, and the stems have pentagonal green leaves with five serrated leaflets. The fruit is shiny black. This plant is abundant in hedgerows near forested areas. It is widespread in Europe and India but has not been seen in Iran. However, it shares medicinal properties similar to the species Rubus saxatilis, which is found in Iran.

8. Blackcurrant

Other names:

Frenge, Ouzumi Galosh, Divanguori.

Latin name:

Black currant.

Scientific Name:

Ribes nigrum L, from the Saxifragaceae family.

Medicinal forms:

Fruit, leaf, stem.

Therapeutic properties and usage:

Blackcurrants have a cool and dry nature and are cooling, laxative, and analgesic. In Germany, its leaves are used as a cold diuretic and cleanser. Infusions of the leaves and stems are beneficial as diuretics and for relieving rheumatism, as an astringent, and in cases of gout, joint swelling, excessive urination, and kidney stones. Additionally, it is helpful in various types of migraines, severe coughs, black cough, and stomach ulcers. Gargling with its infusion is beneficial for relieving throat pain, tonsil inflammation, and stopping gum bleeding. In France, it is common to boil 60-30 grams of dried blackcurrant leaves in one liter of boiling water and consume 3-2 cups per day, with the last cup taken before sleeping. Recently, Swedish researchers have prepared an anti-diarrheal medication called "Pecarin" from blackcurrants. They extract the skin and outer layer of the fruit, which constitutes about 40% of the fruit, dry it, and shape it into pellets. These pellets are known as "Pecarin".[1] Blackcurrant extract is useful for gastrointestinal infections and is usually available in pharmacies in Sweden and other European regions.

Ingredients:

Essential oils are found in the buds and shoots of the plant. The fruit contains malic acid, citric acid, tartaric acid, and pectin. Nopinene, L-sabinene, and D-carvone are found in the essential oil of the buds.

Description:

---

[1]. Pecarin pellets contain a significant amount of anthocyanosides. Anthocyanosides are chemical substances that have antibacterial properties and inhibit the growth of bacteria, especially Escherichia coli, which is the causative agent of diarrhea.

It is another species of blackcurrant. It is a shrub-like plant similar to ordinary blackcurrant, but with the difference that its fruit is black. This plant mostly grows in moist forests and deep forest valleys. It has a wide distribution in Europe, and it is likely to exist in the moist forests of northern Iran, although no exact location reports have been given.

9. Cherry

Other names:

Qarasiya'i, Shirin Karbozbari.

Local names:

Alukok, Helikk, Siahli Halar, Gilahband Haldane.

Latin name:

Cherry.[1]

Scientific name:

Cerasus avium L. Moench, from the Rosaceae family.

Medicinal forms:

Fruit, leaf, gum.

---

1. Cherry trees are called "Cherry tree" in English.

Therapeutic properties and usage:

From a medicinal perspective, when cherry fruit is unripe, it is slightly cold, dry, and astringent. As it becomes half-ripe, red, and sour, it becomes even colder and drier. However, when it fully ripens and becomes sweet, juicy, and dark red or black, it is warm and moist.

In India, cherry fruit is used as an astringent and tonic. It is believed to be beneficial for relieving throat and lung inflammation. However, since it weakens the stomach and makes food acidic, hindering fast digestion, it is recommended not to be consumed immediately after a meal. If consumed shortly after a meal, herbal teas or decoctions made from warm and strengthening plants should be used to aid digestion. Fresh cherries have a laxative effect.

Cherry leaf decoction or infusion acts as a diuretic. To prepare cherry leaf infusion, soak the leaves in cold water for 10-15 hours, then boil 30 parts per thousand of the soaked water, strain it, and consume it as a diuretic. Plum and cherry syrup is prescribed for reducing fever and for individuals with chronic liver and intestinal disorders and edema.[1]

---

1. It is stated in the ancient Greek traditional medicine books that doctors prescribed cherries to treat epilepsy. In the 19th century and in the 1920s and later in America, doctors used black cherry to treat kidney stones and gallbladder problems. In 1950, Dr. Ludig Blue claimed that has treated some patients with gout who were unable to walk and had to use wheelchairs by prescribing them to consume 6 to 8 glasses per day. As long as they continued to consume cherries, their gout remained under control. Recommendations in this regard have also been published in the "Pari va Nashen" journal, and many people with gout have reported that their

Gum:

(Cherry and cherry trees often produce gum, which is called Angum in Persian), most trees of the Rosaceae family, such as peaches, apricots, tomatoes, plums, and cherries, secrete this type of gum, which is yellow in color. It is dark and chemically contains a substance called serazine. The difference between this substance and arabin, which is in gum arabic, is that it does not dissolve in cold water, but when it is boiled, it changes and becomes similar to gum arabic.

Composition:

Barium is present in cherry leaves, and the fruit contains 10-15% sugar. In every 100 grams of raw sweet cherry flesh, the following substances are found: 80 grams of water, 1/3 gram of protein, 3 grams of fat, 17 grams of carbohydrates, 6 grams of ash, 22 milligrams of calcium, 19 milligrams of phosphorus, 4 milligrams of iron, 2 milligrams of sodium, 191 milligrams of potassium, 110 international units of vitamin A, 0.05 milligrams of thiamine, 0.06 milligrams of riboflavin, 4 milligrams of niacin, and 10 milligrams of vitamin C.

---

condition has been controlled by consuming 15 to 20 glasses of red or black cherries daily at the beginning of the treatment, followed by 10 glasses per day.

According to recent experiments, cherry extract has been found to have a strong antibacterial property against dental decay and plaque formation. Black cherry extract inhibits up to 89% of the enzymatic activity responsible for dental plaque formation.

Liquorice gum is considered to have a warm and dry nature and is believed to have the property of eliminating sticky secretions. Therefore, it is beneficial for relieving lung inflammation and also for improving skin complexion, stimulating appetite, breaking down kidney stones, and relieving chronic cough. The recommended dosage is 5 grams. Rubbing it on the skin is useful for improving vision, relieving itching, and treating eyelid scabies, and rubbing it on the skin is used as a cleanser and exfoliator.

Specifications:

This tree is found in Europe and Asia, and in Iran, it grows throughout the northern forests from its length to Gorgan. This tree is a large tree that can reach a height of 20 meters. The bark of the trunk is dark, and the bark of young branches is smooth and green, then turns brown and shiny red. The leaves are egg-shaped with pointed tips and serrated edges. The flowers are white, and the fruit is a small round cherry with a diameter of one centimeter, slightly red or shiny black. The taste of cherries is sour and sweet, and the pit is egg-shaped. Cultivated cherries are large, sweet, juicy, and very delicious. Varieties such as Bigarreaux and Guignes and other sweet varieties have been obtained through selection and breeding work from the wild species Prunus avium, and cherry varieties that are sweet and slightly sour have been obtained by crossing sweet varieties such as Bigarreaux and sour varieties such as Griotte.

10. Clustered Red Currants (Red Gooseberry)

Other names:

Red currants, Garden currants.

Latin names:

Ribes rubrum.

Scientific name:

Ribes rubrum L., from the Saxifragaceae family.

Medicinal forms:

Fruit, leaves, stems.

Therapeutic properties and usage:

The unripe fruit of red currants is appetizing and has a cooling nature, similar to other types of gooseberries. It aids digestion, alleviates inflammation of the digestive system, and acts as a mild laxative. It shares many medicinal properties with other varieties of gooseberries and is consumed as a coolant and diuretic.

Composition:

Fresh leaves of this shrub contain hydrocyanic acid (HCN). Its chemical composition is similar to that of thorny or blade-bearing gooseberries, as mentioned in the relevant section. The fruit of red currants has been reported to contain a coloring substance called cyanidin glycoside.

Preparation of red currant juice:

Clean and chop 20 units of red currants, 2 units of cherries, and 1 unit of plums. Press them on a sieve and let the juice ferment for 24 hours in a cool place. Then strain and preserve the juice or make syrup from it immediately. To prepare a thick red currant syrup, boil 100 units of strained red currant juice with 150 units of sugar and preserve it. Consume it when cooled down. It is recommended not to prepare red currant syrup in a freshly galvanized copper container, as it will acquire an unpleasant taste. The best container for this purpose is enamel or glazed vessels.

Preparation of red currant juice or regular syrup:

Mix 10% unit of thick red currant syrup with 90% unit of water and consume it as a refreshing drink.

Specifications:

It is a shrub similar in size to the thorny gooseberry (Ribes a crispum). Its flowers are white, and its fruit, which grows in clusters, is red, although some varieties have white fruit. The fruit ripens in early summer. This shrub is commonly propagated through cuttings taken from 1-2-year-old branches, which are stored in sand during the winter and planted in their original location or nursery in early spring.

Clustered red currants are native to North Asia and North America. They are cultivated in Iran and are not seen in a wild state.

Ghoreh Ghāt

"Ghoreh Ghāt" is another type of blackcurrant, known as "oriental currant" in English and scientifically named Ribes orientale Dest. It is a thornless shrub with round-toothed leaves and a tapering tip. The back and front of the leaves have glandular hairs. The flowers are yellow, and the fruit is red and vibrant in grape-like clusters covered with small glandular hairs. It is found in the forests of Arasbaran and the southern slopes of the Alborz Mountains in Kurdistan and Rudbar, as well as in the mountains of Hezar-Danesh. A type of Ghoreh Ghāt is also found in the warm waters of Damavand and Ziarat Gorgan. It has laxative properties, and its lint is more abundant than other types of blackcurrants. Sometimes, Ghoreh Ghāt is confused with another plant called "Ghoraqaat," which is different from Ghoreh Ghāt in many aspects.

11. Coconut

Other names:

Narjil, Guzahindi, Ranj.

Latin name:

Coco-Nut.

Scientific name:

Cocos nucifera L, and it belongs to the Palmaceae family.

Medicinal forms:

Fruit core, Milk, Root, Skin.

Therapeutic properties and usage:

Fresh coconut meat is warm and dry, while its dried form is warmer and drier. Coconut milk has a slightly warm and moist nature. It is believed to increase innate heat and promote body weight. It helps eliminate phlegm and excess acidity, and is beneficial for conditions caused by them, such as body weakness, paralysis, melancholia, and similar conditions. It is useful for oral hygiene and beneficial for liver weakness, internal ulcers, hemorrhoids, increasing sperm count, warming the kidneys, relieving back pain, increasing urine secretion, treating bladder coldness, and bladder pain.

Consuming coconut with sugar is blood-building and strengthening. Eating its white meat causes mucus to thicken, delays digestion, and produces thick phlegm, so it should be consumed with sugar. It doesn't have any issues for cold-natured and elderly individuals, and they can eat it without sugar. Those with warm nature should consume it with sour fruits, lemon, and watermelon. The recommended dosage of white meat is up to 14 grams, and for coconut milk, it is up to 100 grams. If eaten with vinegar, which means pickled coconut, the white meat becomes slightly warm and dry, and its properties become laxative. Consuming it is beneficial for expelling various stomach and intestinal worms and pumpkin worms. It is also beneficial for strengthening digestion and rubbing its skin ash on the teeth helps remove plaque.

The oil from coconut meat is beneficial for enhancing understanding, memory, and fat production in the kidneys. It is useful for resolving kidney stones, bladder stones, gas, expelling intestinal worms, and pumpkin worms, reducing back pain, hemorrhoids, and stimulating sexual potency. In China, the root peelings are considered astringent and hemostatic, and they are used for treating bleeding.

In Indonesia, the root is considered antipyretic and diuretic, and it is used for treating and stopping vaginal discharge, urinary tract infections, or bladder discomfort. It is also used for liver ailments.

These fruits are used to treat patients with jaundice, as well as in cases where jaundice is not present. They are mixed with several other roots to treat bronchitis when boiled. In the Malay Peninsula, the boiled root is used as a dressing for infectious diseases. In Indonesia, the decoction of the fruit is used to treat bloody diarrhea, and if it doesn't show effective results after one week, another medicine is prescribed.

In India and China, the fruit's kernel is used as a food ingredient, and it is also consumed in solutions to treat skin diseases, open wounds, and nasal ulcers. In the Malay Peninsula, the leaves of the fruit, along with young coconut milk, are used as diuretics and for the expulsion of kidney stones. Its milk acts as a laxative and is also effective against diarrhea. When the milk is extracted by pressing the flesh, it acts as a laxative for diseases involving blood discharge from the lungs, bloody vomiting, fluid accumulation in body tissues, and intermittent fevers. Additionally, it is used as an antidote for poison throughout Malaysia.[1]

In Java, it is well-known that coconut milk reduces human fertility, so people are cautious about consuming it. The ash of the coconut husk mixed with wine is effective in treating specific stages of syphilis. Its charcoal is a good absorbent, and the pure

---

1. During World War I, the charcoal was used to absorb gas in gas masks

oil obtained from distilling its flesh is very useful for treating dental diseases. Furthermore, it is used as a container for mixing other medicines, such as oil ointments.[1]

Composition:

Coconut contains oxidase and catalase enzymes. Its milk contains specific amino acids: histidine, arginine, lysine, tyrosine, tryptophan, proline, leucine, and alanine. Its oil, which constitutes about 57-75% of the flesh, contains lauric acid, myristic acid, other fatty acids, phytosterols, and squalene. Additionally, it contains a mannose from the coconut kernel.

A galactomannan soluble in water is found in it. Another report states that coconut contains fixed oil, volatile oil, and wax, including myricyl ester of cerotic acid. The flesh contains proteins, vitamins A, B, and C, nonyl alcohol, methyl heptyl ketone, methyl undecyl ketone, caproic acid, decanoic acid, caprylic acid, lauric acid, myristic acid, and stearic acid. It also contains lecithin, stigmasterol, choline, globulin, galactoarabinan, and galactomannan. The coconut water or coconut milk contains protein, ash, sucrose, oxidase, catalase, and diastase. In every 100 grams of fresh coconut meat, the following substances are present: water 50.9 grams, protein 3.5

---

1. many other countless properties have been attributed to coconut, with a superstitious aspect, among the native people of coconut-growing regions, which are not scientifically proven.

grams, fat 35 grams, carbohydrates 9 grams, calcium 13 milligrams, phosphorus 95 milligrams, iron 1.7 milligrams, sodium 23 milligrams, potassium 256 milligrams, thiamine 0.05 milligrams, riboflavin 0.02 milligrams, and vitamin C 0.1 milligrams.

In every 100 grams of dried coconut meat, the following substances are present: water 3.5 grams, protein 7.2 grams, fat 65 grams, carbohydrates 23 grams, calcium 26 milligrams, phosphorus 178 milligrams, iron 3.3 milligrams, potassium 588 milligrams, vitamin A zero, thiamine 0.06 milligrams, riboflavin 0.04 milligrams, niacin 0.6 milligrams, and vitamin C zero.

In every 100 grams of coconut milk, the following substances are present: water 65 grams, protein 3.2 grams, fat 25 grams, carbohydrates 5 grams, calcium 16 milligrams, phosphorus 100 milligrams, iron 1.6 milligrams, thiamine 0.03 milligrams, riboflavin trace amounts, niacin 0.8 milligrams, and vitamin C 2 milligrams.

Specifications:

The coconut tree is a large tree that can reach a height of 20-25 meters, and its trunk diameter can reach up to one meter. The trunk is straight and upright, with visible traces of shed leaves on it. At the end of the trunk, usually around 14 tree leaves can be seen. The leaves are large, measuring 4-5 meters in length, and composed of numerous long and narrow leaflets. The color of the leaves is light green. The terminal bud of the tree is a source of food that is consumed by the local people. The coconut tree usually starts to bear fruits around the fifth year. The flowers are male and female, found in clusters on the same tree. A coconut tree produces approximately 5,060 coconuts per year, which amounts to around 6-5 thousand coconuts per hectare. From these fruits, about one ton of coconut kernel, known as copra in trade, is obtained.

On average, about 60% of copra consists of fatty substances, oil, or coconut butter, which are extracted and sold in the market. Coconut trees can be easily propagated through seed cultivation. The seeds are planted in nurseries, and after 4-5 months, young coconut plants emerge. After one year, they are transplanted to their final location with a spacing of 10x10 meters. However, it requires rich and prepared soil.

The coconut tree is specifically suited for tropical regions such as Sri Lanka, India, the Philippines, New Caledonia, China, and other tropical areas. In Iran, coconuts are imported, and a few trees have been planted in Chabahar.

12. Cornelian Cherry

Other names:

Zaqal Qaranya, Qarn Hab al-Shum.

Latin name:

Dogberry.

Scientific name:

Cornus mas, and it belongs to the Cornaceae family, genus Cornus.

Medicinal Properties and usage:

Cornelian cherry has a slightly cool and moderate nature, but it is dry and astringent. It is beneficial for treating diarrhea, healing stomach ulcers, strengthening the stomach, relieving thirst, and reducing inflammation of the stomach, liver, blood, and bile. It is also good for respiratory health, and it is recommended to consume it with sugar.

The fruit of the cornelian cherry has a pleasant taste, dark red or blackish sour, resembling plum or olive. When the fruit is raw, it is green, but it turns colorful after ripening. The skin of the cornelian cherry tree contains about 7-8% tannin, pectic substances, malic acid, and two types of calcium salts. The flower of the tree contains a substance called quercetin, and the fruit contains glucose and sucrose sugars, as well as glycolic acid. Additionally, the fruit has abundant pulp.

Specifications:

Cornelian cherry is a small tree that grows up to 8 meters in height, with a trunk diameter of 15-19 centimeters. Its young branches are yellowish-green, and the skin is brownish-yellow. The leaves are ovate with pointed tips, rounded bases, and pale undersides. The leaf blade is 8 cm long and 3-7 cm wide, with a short petiole. The small yellow flowers appear early in spring. The fruit is firm, similar in size and shape to an olive, and has a dark red color. The tree grows in mixed forests, particularly in the Arasbaran region of Iran. When local residents cut down the forest, they take away the other trees except for the cornelian cherry, which they keep in its original location to use its fruit. This tree attracts honey bees due to its abundant nectar. It also grows in Europe, Armenia, and the Caucasus.

13. Cornus

Other names:

Miran.

Latin name:

Bloody-dog-wood, Female-Cornel, Dog berry.

Scientific name:

Cornus Sanguinea L from the family Cornace.

Medicinal forms:

Fruits, Stem Bark.

Therapeutic properties and usage:

The fruit and stem bark of the Cornus tree have antipyretic effects.

Ingredients:

The fruit of the Cornus tree is edible, and in addition to calcium malate, it contains a green-colored substance. Its seeds contain 15-20% extractable oil, which has antipyretic properties when used medicinally.

Plant Specifications:

Cornus is a small shrub that does not exceed 4-5 meters in height. Its branches are purplish, and the bark of its trunk is brown with a pungent odor. Its leaves are ovate with a pointed tip, green on the top and pale green on the back, about 4-10 centimeters long, with relatively long leaf stalks, and turn into dark purple in autumn. Its flowers are small, and its fruit is very small, round, with a diameter of 5-8 millimeters, and black in color. This shrub produces abundant suckers and reproduces rapidly naturally. The root, bark, and flowers of this plant have an unpleasant odor.

This plant grows in mountainous regions of Europe, East Asia, and Iran. In Iran, it grows in the mountains of Shahou, Kurdistan, and Arasbaran in forests.

14. Cucumber[1]

Other names:

Qitha.

Scientific name:

Cucumber, Cucumis sativus L.

Family:

Cucurbitaceae.

Medicinal forms:

Seeds, fruit, roots, leaves.

Medicinal properties and usage:

---

1. A type of cucumber called "Chenbar" has a long, thin, white-to-light green, striped and grooved appearance. In Persian, it is known as "Chenbar cucumber" or "Neyshaburi cucumber", and its properties are similar to regular cucumbers.

Cucumber seeds have cooling, strengthening, and diuretic properties. Consuming cucumber soup relieves thirst and opens up constricted and blocked urine.

Pulverized cucumber ointment is very useful for skin discomfort, burns from fire, and burns from boiling water.

Boiled dried cucumber roots are diuretic and beneficial for treating beriberi. The juice of crushed leaves of cucumber is used as a gastric tonic for children with digestive disorders. In India and China, green and unripe cucumbers cooked with sugar are given to children with bloody diarrhea. In Indonesia, the fruit and its extract are used for treating Sprue and are beneficial. Cucumber fruit extract is useful for treating bladder stones.[1]

Cucumber is relatively cool and moist in nature, and its flesh is moister than its skin. It is recommended to consume the lower part of the cucumber, where it is attached to the plant. It relieves thirst and alleviates heat in the blood, bile, and inflammation. It is beneficial for warm stomachs and bladder pain. It is a laxative and diuretic, beneficial for the expulsion of bladder and kidney stones. In these cases, the bitter part of the cucumber is more beneficial.

Cucumber is a bloating vegetable and quickly spoils in the stomach. It should not be consumed with hard-to-digest foods. If

---

1. Sprue is a rare disease found in most tropical countries and sometimes in temperate regions. Its distinctive symptoms include weight loss, loss of muscle mass, various irregularities, and digestive disorders, especially malabsorption of fats, glucose, and vitamins. The main cause and specific agent of the disease have not yet been identified.

cooked, it spoils faster in the stomach compared to when eaten raw. That's why cucumber should be consumed with salt. Cucumber seeds have diuretic properties and act as a cleanser and opener for the veins due to their mucilaginous substances. Applying cucumber water on the skin externally relieves itching and skin irritations. Cucumber water is used in the preparation of various cosmetic products. A paste made from cucumber water, beeswax, and honey is very effective in smoothing and soothing the skin and treating acne. Cucumber seeds have anti-worm properties.

Components:

Cucumber fruit contains small amounts of saponin, an enzyme called proteolytic enzyme, and glutathione.

Further analysis shows that cucumber fruit contains proteolytic enzyme, ascorbic acid oxidase, succinic dehydrogenase, and malic dehydrogenase. The fragrant substance in cucumber can be extracted with alcohol. Additionally, cucumber contains the enzyme erpase. Vitamin B1 and C are also found in cucumber.

In every 100 grams of cucumber, the following components are present: water 95 grams, protein 0.9 grams, fat 1 gram, carbohydrates 2.5 grams, ash 0.5 grams, phosphorus 27 milligrams, iron 1.1 milligrams, calcium 25 milligrams, potassium 160 milligrams, vitamin A 250 international units, sodium 6 milligrams, thiamine 0.03 milligrams, riboflavin 0.04 milligrams, niacin 0.2 milligrams, and vitamin C 11 milligrams.

Characteristics:

Cucumber is an annual herbaceous plant with trailing stems covered in firm and rough hairs. It has large serrated leaves, and its flowers are large and yellow, with separate male and female flowers on the same plant. Its fruit is green, white, small, or large, depending on the different varieties. Small, unripe green cucumbers are harvested and consumed, while larger fruits are used in the perfume industry.

In Iran, various cucumber varieties are grown and produced on a large scale, so the cultivation method is diverse.

15. Date Palm

Date palm is known by various names, including "Khorma" and "Tamr" in Persian. Its Latin name is Phoenix dactylifera.

Scientific name:

Phoenix dactylifera L, and it belongs to the Palmaceae family.

Medicinal forms:

Fruit, seed, gum, and pollen.

Therapeutic Properties and Usage:

Date palm is considered to have a warm and slightly dry nature, although some varieties are considered cool and moist. It is believed to have properties similar to other fruits such as figs, pomegranates, jujubes, and mulberries. Boiling 50 grams of date palm in 1000 grams of water and then straining it creates a highly effective syrup for relieving chest congestion and softening the chest.

It is beneficial for paralysis, kidney strengthening, relieving lower back pain, and is suitable for individuals with a cool temperament. Consuming boiled date palm with fenugreek is useful for phlegmatic fevers and breaking down kidney stones. If the dates are soaked in fresh milk with a bit of cinnamon and consumed, followed by drinking some milk afterward, it is effective for enhancing sexual potency. Date palm is heavy to digest and slow in digestion, so it is not suitable for people with a warm temperament. Date palm is generally not suitable for residents of non-date-growing regions. It can cause liver and spleen congestion, disruption of bodily humors, headaches, toothaches, and mouth ulcers. To alleviate these symptoms, consuming pomegranate, scallion, and skinless almonds can be helpful. After consuming date palm in such non-date-growing climates, rinsing the mouth with lukewarm water soaked with sumac or vinegar, and eventually chewing tarragon for a while can prevent the occurrence of these symptoms.

The date palm seed is warm and dry, and its consumption is highly astringent. Consuming the boiled seed is beneficial for breaking down kidney stones, and applying its powder is useful for treating diarrhea. The burnt ashes of the seed can be used to heal malignant ulcers. In India, the gum of the date palm tree is used for diarrhea and treating reproductive and urinary tract diseases. Seedless date fruits are consumed for softening the chest, as a laxative for asthma and chest discomfort, and for relieving cough. They are also used for fever and burns.

It has been revealed in recent studies that date palm pollen stimulates the sexual glands in both men and women. Consuming 10 grams of date palm pollen extract noticeably increases the weight of the ovaries in women and the testicles in men. This is why tarragon extract is prepared and valued. Additionally, date palm is consumed to enhance sexual potency.

Moreover, it is consumed for increasing sexual potency. Recent studies have shown that date palm seeds, when pollinated, stimulate the sexual glands in both men and women. Consuming 10 grams of date palm pollen extract significantly increases the weight of the ovaries in women and the testes in men. This is why tarragon extract is prepared and valued.

The ripe date or "tamr" contains a significant amount of carbohydrates (approximately 70-65%), with about 25% sucrose, 45% glucose, and other carbon hydrates. Additionally, it contains viscous substances, various vitamins such as vitamin E, A, B, D, a considerable amount of potassium (648 milligrams per 100 grams), and small amounts of other minerals.

In every 100 grams of edible part of raw and dried dates, the following substances are present: water (22 grams), protein (2.2 grams), fat (0.5 grams), carbohydrates (72 grams), ash (1.9 grams), calcium (59 milligrams), phosphorus (63 milligrams), iron (3 milligrams), sodium (1 milligram), potassium (648 milligrams), vitamins (50 international units), thiamine (0.09 milligrams), riboflavin (0.1 milligrams), niacin (2.2 milligrams).

Specifications:

The date palm tree can reach a height of 10 to 30 meters and has a straight, unbranched, cylindrical trunk with remnants of old leaf bases. Its leaves are feather-like, thorny, and can reach a length of 6 to 3 meters, with a dark green color and a rough and waxy texture.

The date palm tree is dioecious, meaning some trees are male and some are female. If the tree is grown from seeds, the female flowers appear after ten years, and the tree starts to bear fruit. However, if the tree is grown from offshoots, which is more common, it starts bearing fruit after 4-5 years. In the early stages, the female flowers are enclosed in a brownish plant tissue chamber, and after the female flowers are pollinated with pollen from male trees, which is obtained from male date palms, the fruits gradually appear. Farmers have named the seven stages of date fruit development, which are:

1. Talleh, which is the spring of the date fruit.
2. The male flower in spring is called "Goshn," and it is also called "Tarooneh". In Shiraz, it is common to extract the juice of Tarooneh at the Talleh stage and sell it in the market.
3. The pollinated female flowers are called "Balkh".
4. Ghooreh is the unripe date, which is still green and not yet sweet.
5. Besar: The ripe date, which has turned yellow.
6. Qosb, which in Persian refers to the stone-breaking date, and the people of Shiraz call it "Ghosbak".
7. Fresh and ripe dates that are slightly drier than rotab.

Each of these stages has relatively different medicinal properties.

The ripe date fruit, depending on the type, can have light brown, brown, or dark brown colors. It has a fleshy, sweet interior with a long seed measuring 3-1 centimeters in length and 2-5 millimeters in diameter. It appears in the form of large clusters. In some varieties, the seed is so small that it is almost invisible. Date palms are propagated through planting offshoots, which are obtained from the base of the tree. These offshoots, weighing 10-15 kilograms, are planted in their original location in spring with a distance of 7 to 8 meters from each side, and usually, one female offshoot is planted for every three male offshoots.

Dates are native to tropical regions of Africa and Arabia and are also cultivated in other warm regions of the world. In Iran, they are grown in all warm regions of the country, including various areas in Khuzestan, Kerman, Fars, Baluchistan, and central regions.

16. Fig

Other names:

Teen (Persian).

Latin name:

Fig tree.

Scientific name:

Ficus carica L. belongs to the Moraceae family.

Medicinal forms:

Fruit, syrup, leaves.

Therapeutic properties and usage:

According to its nature, fig is considered warm and moist. It is believed to have laxative, diuretic, antipyretic, and thirst-quenching properties. It is also said to strengthen sexual potency, cool the heart, relieve obstructions, strengthen the liver, and alleviate spleen swelling and hemorrhoids. It helps relieve low urine secretion and is beneficial for relieving aggression, chest pain, cough, and lung inflammation.[1] If consumed fresh or dried with the kernel of a yellow flower and a little borax (75% warm), it acts as a strong laxative for thick phlegm. A poultice made from dried fig, barley flour, and wheat is useful for resolving ear swelling and abscesses. Its decoction, when mixed with plantain, is very beneficial for chest pain and chest inflammation, and if the decoction is purified with a filter cloth, it is useful for relieving heartburn.[2]

The poultice of fig, when combined with chamomile, is good for cold gout, and the poultice of fig syrup and barley flour is beneficial for skin ulcers or wounds. Furthermore, rubbing fig helps prevent hair loss. If figs are soaked in vinegar for 9 days and consumed daily, 5 figs each day with vinegar, and some of them are crushed and applied as a poultice, it is very good for resolving spleen swelling.[3]

It is harmful for weak livers so peoples with weak livers should consume figs with walnuts. The dosage ranges from 150 grams for dried figs to 450 grams for fresh figs. Fig coffee is prescribed

---

1. Take 50 grams of yellow figs and boil them in 500 grams of milk for 15 minutes, strain it, and sweeten it according to the patient's taste. This syrup is very beneficial for throat swelling. Mix equal amounts of four fruits: date, seedless persimmon, dried fig, and raisin, and coat them with powdered sugar.
2. Take three stalks and four leaves of plantain, boil them in a sufficient amount of water, and after straining, obtain 500 grams of the decoction. This decoction is beneficial for softening the breasts and relieving breast pain.
3. Fig stem sap, especially from unripe fruit, is a white-colored plant sap that comes out due to fruit pressure or breaking branches. Its taste is sour, slightly bitter, and pungent, and it is usually used to remove warts, provided that vinegar does not have specific side effects for the patient.

for pulmonary diseases, acute conditions, bronchitis, and chronic cough.

In traditional medicine of the Far East, which has spread to the Western world, it is stated that fig fruit is a mild laxative and aids digestion. In China, they cook slightly unripe figs in meat soup, which is very nutritious and increases milk secretion. Fig leaves are slightly toxic, but if boiled in boiling water until vapor is released, the resulting decoction is beneficial for swollen and painful hemorrhoids. Other scholars have only mentioned the use of fig leaves for treating hemorrhoids, and they use fig leaf syrup[1] and decoction for treating hemorrhoids. Fig leaf decoction is good for relieving stomach pain, and if poured over hemorrhoids, it is beneficial.[2]

Fig syrup is beneficial for gum inflammation, hemorrhoids, and tonsillitis. The dissolved syrup of boiled fig leaves acts as an insecticide.

Composition:

In its fruit, fig contains sugars, nitrogenous compounds, a small amount of fat, minerals, proteins, amino acids, tryptophan, carotene, lipase protease enzyme, and keravine. In its leaves, approximately 0.06% of fucosin, a bitter substance, and

---

[1]. The white fig syrup, similar to ficine, is highly poisonous and has a cell-destroying effect on the skin and epidermis.
[2]. To prepare it, figs are dried and roasted like coffee.

beragaptene can be found. Proteolytic enzymes are separated from its white sap.

Other studies have reported the following compounds in fig:

In the fruit, fig contains sugar, invert sugar, tartaric acid, malic acid, citric acid, phenolics, and vitamin A. The dried fig seed contains fixed oil and a small amount of boric acid.

Fig leaves contain pepsin, urease, papain, tyrosine, and glucomannan, phytosterol, serotinic acid, and sitosterol. A routine extract is obtained from the leaves of this plant, which contains coumarin, tannins, and rhamnose.

Research in India has shown that the leaves of this plant contain fucosin and a small amount of bergapten. Scientific studies have shown that figs have medicinal properties for treating vitiligo or leukoderma. Therefore, this medication, similar to what is found in Psoralea corylifolia L, also has beneficial effects in the treatment of vitiligo.

In every 100 grams of dried raw figs, the following substances are present: 23 grams of water, 4.3 grams of protein, 0.3 grams of fat, 69 grams of carbohydrates (sugars, starch, and cellulose), 126 milligrams of calcium, 77 milligrams of phosphorus, 3 milligrams of iron, 34 milligrams of sodium, 640 milligrams of potassium, 80 international units of vitamin E, 0.10 milligrams of thiamine, 10 milligrams of riboflavin, and 7 milligrams of niacin.

Specifications:

The fig is a plant that originated from the East and has been cultivated in Mediterranean regions for centuries. It is a small tree that reaches a height of 5 to 6 meters, sometimes slightly more. Its large, palmate leaves are divided into 5 parts and resemble rough, grayish-green hair.

From a botanical perspective, the fig fruit is not a typical fruit but rather a type of floral enclosure or inflorescence that contains male and female flowers. When the fruit ripens, the female flowers, the floral cup, and the lower part of it become fleshy and edible.

The fig tree is not resistant to severe cold and cannot tolerate temperatures below 15 degrees Celsius below freezing. It grows in most soils, preferably rich ones. Its propagation is mostly done through cuttings, and sometimes by layering its branches. Fig cuttings are usually prepared in February from 2-3-year-old branches, about 60-70 centimeters long. For this purpose, strong and healthy trees should be selected. These cuttings develop roots shortly after planting and after 4-5 years, they form a productive tree. However, strong root suckers from old trees can also be used, and after a few years, when they have been planted, they are grafted.

To take care of fig trees, agricultural practices such as plowing the orchard soil and fertilizing the trees are essential for their growth. Fig fruits are usually harvested twice a year, once in summer and once in autumn. Autumn harvest is usually selected for drying figs. Fig trees start bearing fruit from 3 to 5 years old and continue to bear fruit until 20 years old. After that, rejuvenation measures should be taken.

Fig trees grow in vast areas of forests in northern Iran, Azerbaijan, Isfahan, around Tehran, Shiraz, Khuzestan Dalki, Khorasan, and western regions of Iran. Various wild fig varieties are found in Iranian forests.

Ficus carica L. var genuina Boiss, known as the Domestic fig or Common fig tree, is found in coastal forests of the Caspian Sea and in the forests of Arasbaran and Golestan. It grows up to 6 meters in height, and its fruit is small and sweet. An interesting fact about this fig is that it sometimes grows as an epiphyte on other trees like the mulberry. Its roots enter the trunk of the host tree and descend downwards to reach the ground. It is locally known as "Divoonjir" in Mazandaran, "Hanjir" in Kurdistan, and "Kar" in Lorestan. Its properties are similar to those of cultivated figs.

Ficus carica L. var johannis Boiss grows wild in Tabas, Balochistan, Fars, and the Takht-e-Jamshid Mountains up to 1500 meters above sea level. Its fruit is small, slightly velvety, and its properties are more or less similar to cultivated figs.

Ficus carica L. var rupestris Haussk: This fig grows in western Iran, in Lorestan, Arak, Kohgiluyeh, and Fars. Its fruit is pear-shaped and somewhat wrinkled.

17. Grapefruit

Latin name:

Grapefruit and Pomelo.

Scientific name:

Citrus paradisi Macf from the Rutaceae citrus family.[1]

Medicinal properties:

Fruit peel.

Therapeutic properties and usage:

In India, grapefruit juice is used to increase the body's resistance against colds, and consuming grapefruit enhances the body's resistance against the spread and discomfort of infected wounds.

Other properties, especially the peel, resemble the characteristics of C.grandis or Sultan citrus species.

---

1. Some botanists believe that grapefruit originated from a mutation of another citrus called "Tosabz" and consider it a hybrid of "Tosabz" (C.decumana).

Ingredients:

It contains compounds such as pectin, limonene, sesquiterpenes, aldehydes, juvabione, caryophyllene, and oxygenated compounds.

In addition to the peel, the essence of grapefruit is extracted from the leaves and green stems of grapefruit varieties used for consumption.

In every 100 grams of edible grapefruit, the following nutrients are present:

Water: 88 grams.

Protein: 5 grams.

Energy: 41 kilocalories.

Fat: 0.1 grams.

Carbohydrates: 10.6 grams.

Calcium: 16 milligrams.

Iron: 0.4 milligrams.

Sodium: 1 milligram.

Potassium: 135 milligrams.

Vitamin A: 80 International Units.

Thiamine: 0.04 milligrams.

Riboflavin: 0.02 milligrams.

Niacin: 0.2 milligrams.

Vitamin C: 38 milligrams.

Phosphorus: 16 milligrams.

Characteristics:

It is a medium-sized, thorny tree with simple, leathery, complete leaves, ovoid with pointed tips and wavy edges. Its flowers are white and resemble other citrus varieties. Its fruit is large, much larger than an orange. When mature, its peel is thin, initially green, and after ripening, it turns bright yellow, shiny, and smooth due to sulfur. If it exceeds the ripeness stage and is not picked, its peel becomes thick and spongy, and the white sponge inside the peel becomes thick, and the edible part becomes less juicy. Ripe fruit has watery pulp, pale yellow in color, with a sour or sweet and slightly bitter and delicate taste. A type of grapefruit with red pulp is called "Sorkh" (Red) in northern Iran.

Grapefruit is cultivated in China, India, and Middle Eastern regions such as Greece, Palestine, Syria, and Iran. In Iran, it is mainly grown in northern and southern regions of the country.[1]

---

1. "Tosabz": Another type of citrus that appears to be the primary origin of grapefruit and has emerged as a result of sudden changes and genetic mutations in grapefruit. Its shape is slightly elongated and pear-shaped, with the flesh or peel color being green, and its taste is very sour and juicy, with the edible part being fibrous and coarse. Its skin is thick and cottony, and the outer surface is uneven and yellow. Tosabz is also known as "Beshghabi" in northern Iran, and its scientific name is Citrus deumana Murray var piriformia.

18. Grapes

Other names:

Moushatak, Rostanak, Tank, Warm, Anab, Wild grape, Boodaveh, Ambasluqi, Warm Berry, Divorz and Teleh, Ruz, Ghoreh Miu, Rash, and Tarrash.

Latin name:

Grape or Vine Tree.

Scientific Name:

Vitis sylvestris Gmel (from the Vitaceae family).

Medicinal parts:

Fruit, Leaves, Seeds.

Therapeutic properties and usage:

Grapes are considered warm and moist in nature, and it is believed to balance the bodily humors. They are highly nutritious and blood-building, cleansing the blood from impurities and toxins. Grapes are beneficial for the chest and lungs. It is recommended to remove the skin of grapes before consuming them, especially for grapes with thick skin, as the skin is difficult to digest and can cause stomach discomfort. Grape juice is harmful for individuals with wet and bloating stomachs as it creates gas and bloating. In such cases, it should be consumed with thyme and caraway seeds. It is also harmful for liver and spleen congestion and kidney bloating, and in these cases, it should be consumed with celery seeds. Grapes give rise to thirst and should be eaten with sour foods to quench the thirst because consuming cold water after grapes can cause its spoilage in the stomach and lead to water retention and infectious fevers. Excessive and continuous consumption of grape juice can lead to kidney stones.

(1) Grapes should not be eaten immediately after harvesting and it is better to consume them after 1-2 days. Fresh grapes have a laxative and diuretic effect. Leftover grapes with withered skin are more beneficial and cause less bloating. They have better properties and are safer compared to fresh grapes. Grapes strengthen the body, increase the production of healthy blood, and have a beneficial effect on chronic fevers and colds. They are easily digested and beneficial for chest and lung diseases.

Raisins and currants are better in all aspects and are beneficial for the stomach, liver, kidneys, bladder, and chest.[1]

Grape seed oil is highly emollient, warming to the body, and softens the skin. Grape seeds, in terms of nature, are cold and dry, and due to their tannin content, they have astringent properties, because bloating, tighten the stomach, and reduce urine and sperm secretion. Grape seeds are harmful to the bladder and kidneys. Grape skins, in terms of nature, are cold and dry, and they are difficult to digest and remain in the folds and wrinkles of the intestines, causing bloating and gas. Dried grape skin is beneficial for most wounds. Therefore, when eating fresh grapes, it is advisable to chew the skin as much as possible and discard it. Grape leaf is strengthening, astringent, and diuretic. A decoction of 30 grams of grape leaves in 1000 grams of water is used to treat diarrhea, prevent excessive bleeding, urine disorders, gout, jaundice, and varicose veins. Green and young grape tendrils have similar properties to grape leaves, and they are usually consumed alone or mixed with grape leaf extract in a daily amount of 30-50 grams to prevent internal bleeding and treat simple diarrhea or bloody diarrhea.

Ghoreh (unripe grape):

---

1. To prepare grape seed oil, press the seeds, boil the resulting juice and residue with olive oil, and strain it to obtain a clear oil.

In traditional medicine books, it is referred to as "Hasroom" and in English, it is called "Unripe grape". It is cold and astringent in nature and is used for treating mouth mucous membrane inflammation and softening the gums. Ghoreh water is beneficial for preventing excessive obesity and combating scurvy or vitamin C deficiency. Due to the presence of potassium bitartrate, it is highly beneficial for sciatica and acute rheumatism.

Vinegar:

In traditional medicine books, it is referred to as "Khall" and in English, it is called "Vinegar". It is a sour liquid obtained by fermenting wine and is essentially a diluted and natural form of acetic acid.

Vinegar refers to all liquid substances that have undergone alcoholic fermentation and have been converted into acetic acid. Vinegar is obtained industrially by fermenting wine. In addition to acetic acid, vinegar contains malic acid, tartaric acid, potassium acid tartrate, lime, and a small amount of coloring matter.

Vinegar is considered cool and dry in nature, and it is believed to have astringent and moisture-drying properties. It penetrates quickly and cuts through thick mixtures. Applying vinegar alone or mixed with olive oil is beneficial for relieving headaches, sunburn-related headaches, headaches caused by bile, or headaches caused by hot baths. Applying a vinegar compress or a rosewater and vinegar compress to the forehead is beneficial and helpful for the mentioned conditions. Diluted vinegar gargle is also useful for throat inflammation and sore throat. Mixing vinegar with honey and applying it to the skin in the area of bruising helps accelerate the absorption of the bruise. Placing a drop of vinegar in the ear is an effective remedy for relieving ear pain and consuming vinegar orally is beneficial for tinnitus, hearing loss, opening clogged ears, and strengthening hearing. Consuming vinegar orally is also helpful for internal bleeding cessation, aiding digestion, stimulating appetite, cutting through gall bladder obstructions, removing urinary blockages, and facilitating the effect of medicines on the spleen. Regular fasting consumption of vinegar is beneficial for eliminating stomach worms. Applying vinegar is beneficial for burns, preventing the spread of infected and bad wounds, ulcerated eczema, body itchiness, and relieving the sting of poisonous animals. Pouring vinegar on the affected area is useful for preventing external bleeding and cutting off its flow.

Traditional method of vinegar preparation:

Preparing vinegar is very simple. Take grape juice, strain it, or without straining, put the crushed grape residues inside a ceramic or china jug or barrel. In the traditional method, it was customary to rub the inner part of the jug with pitch, then pour 10% of the weight of grape juice in clean vinegar and tightly cover the jug.

Place it in the sun in a warm place until it is ready. Another method is not to add vinegar from the beginning and wait until the grape juice boils, then add vinegar and salt and let it reach acidity or let it naturally turn into wine.

The harms of vinegar are for the elderly, weak-bodied individuals, and patients suffering from Unripe walnut pickles are also very beneficial. To prepare it, pick unripe walnuts when they are about the size of a hazelnut, soak them in vinegar, and let them ripen until they become pickles.

"Faghah Al-Karam," which is the blossom of the grapevine, is cool, dry, and fragrant in nature. The best type of it is the fresh blossoms from wild grapes. It strengthens the stomach, relieves hiccups, and if its extract is distilled, it becomes even stronger and more effective.

In China, grapevine roots are used as a calming agent for hiccups and diuretic, as well as for increasing milk secretion and treating infertility. Grapes are used as a tonic, diuretic, and antileptic, as well as for treating stones.

In India, they rub the juice of green and young grapevine branches on the skin to treat skin diseases. Grape leaves have astringent properties and are used to stop diarrhea. Grape juice or grape water is consumed as an astringent for throat and throat discomfort. Raisins are consumed as a coolant, laxative, tonic, for relieving thirst, reducing body heat, stopping severe coughing, and strengthening.

Dibs (grape syrup) is called "Doushab" in Persian. It is obtained from the concentrated juice of grapes, dates, or mulberries. Respiratory diseases such as fresh and dry cough, chest pain, weakness of organs and abdominal organs, sexual power, and harmful uterus are detrimental to the nerves, sexual power, and melancholic temperament. Constant consumption of such food leads to weakness, impaired vision, yellowing of the complexion, and weight loss. To avoid these side effects, individuals in need can consume vinegar with sweets and fatty broth. In cases of cough, they can consume sweets with almond oil and mild-heat medications. In cases of nerve weakness, it is recommended to use honey and warm spices as a remedy. The recommended dosage is up to 35 grams, and in some cases, lemon juice can be used instead of vinegar.

The absolute meaning refers to grape juice and dates. To make grape juice at home, ripe grape juice is extracted and strained, then boiled until three-fourths of it evaporates and one-fourth remains. After that, a special type of soil, similar to clay, is added and left to settle to enhance sweetness. If soil is not added, it will have a sour taste and be somewhat uneven. The grape juice without soil is usually referred to as grape syrup. As for date juice and mulberry juice, the customary method is to boil the ripe fruit in boiling water to extract its sweetness. Then it is strained and heated until it thickens. Another type is called "triangle," which is grape juice that is boiled and reduced to two-thirds, leaving one-third remaining. Avicenna's Canon of Medicine refers to this method as a legitimate one, where grape juice is mixed with water in a ratio of 3 parts grape juice to 1 part water, then boiled until one-third of it evaporates, and the rest remains. Another type mentioned in the book "Tuḥfe-i Ḥakīm-i Mu'min" is called "Manṣaf," which is grape juice where half of it evaporates during boiling and the other half remains. It has similar properties to the triangle mixture.

Grape juice is considered a blood tonic and digestive tonic. It is beneficial for individuals suffering from smallpox, measles, and chest congestion. It is beneficial for individuals with a melancholic temperament. Excessive consumption of grape juice by hot-tempered individuals is harmful. From a natural perspective, grape juice is warm and moist, and it acts as a blood tonic and weight-gainer. It opens up clogged and constricted blood vessels. It is beneficial when consumed with vinegar for epilepsy and with fumitory for fear, anxiety, and madness. Consuming almond kernel water is beneficial for controlling dysentery. Consuming it with figs and purslane is beneficial for chronic cough and chest pain. Consuming it with a little saffron is very beneficial for relieving palpitations and weakness in the abdominal organs. Mixing it with boiled barley is good for breaking down bladder and kidney stones, and it is highly diuretic. The cooked dressing of grape juice with khame is effective for reducing inflammation and opening up closed abscesses. The recommended dosage is between 100 to 10 grams. Excessive consumption leads to blood burning and exacerbates headaches, especially in hot-tempered individuals. To alleviate these symptoms, basil seeds and poppy seeds can be used.

Raisin:

In traditional books, it is referred to as "Zabib" (raisin). Raisin is a type of grape that is dried on the vine or, more accurately, semi-dried. The best type of raisin is the one with few-seeded or seedless, fleshy grapes, while the weakest and least desirable type is the one with dried, less fleshy, and seeded grapes. In terms of nature, raisin varies slightly depending on the type of grape and the method of preparation. Raisin made from white grapes has less warmth compared to the one made from black grapes. Very sweet raisin has more warmth than less sweet raisin. Raisin is dry and astringent with dry and warm properties. Raisin seeds are naturally warm and dry. In terms of properties, it is believed that raisin balances thick humors and has a mild laxative nature. It aids in the absorption and effectiveness of laxative medications, is beneficial for lung cleansing, strengthens the liver, and stimulates the sexual power of cold-tempered individuals. It is also beneficial for phlegm cough, kidney and bladder diseases, and intestinal ulcers. If it is soaked and eaten with borage flower and fresh dates, it is beneficial for palpitations. It is useful for jaundice when consumed with vinegar. If raisin seeds are removed and replaced with peppercorns and eaten, it is very beneficial for relieving kidney and bladder coldness, urinary retention, and drop by drop urination. If raisin is cooked with anise and eaten with almond oil, it is beneficial for relieving cold and phlegm-induced cough. Soaking raisin in water or cooking it with suitable laxative medications has a moistening nature. If soaked in grape vinegar and eaten on an empty stomach, it is beneficial for resolving spleen swelling. In this way, every day for a while, eating a few raisin seeds soaked in vinegar and drinking some vinegar along with it. Raisin dressing with animal fat is beneficial for resolving swelling and opening abscesses. Its dressing with wine is beneficial for carbuncles, dirty wounds, smallpox sores, joint infections, and boils. Similarly, its dressing with chickpea flour and cumin is beneficial for testicular swelling. Raisin is harmful for warm-tempered individuals, so it should be consumed with mint and/or sour fruits and poppy seeds. It is harmful for the kidneys, so it should be consumed with jujube. The recommended intake of raisin is up to 120 grams, and its substitute in terms of properties is raisins.

Raisin seeds are cold and dry and have a stomach-binding effect. They are beneficial for strengthening weak and loose stomachs. Thin and less fleshy raisins also have a stomach-binding effect. They burn the blood, and they should be consumed with purslane or fennel seeds."

Ingredients

A grape cluster generally consists of the following parts:

In the stem of the grape cluster, the following substances are identified:

Tannin: 2-1%.

Resinous materials: 1-1.5%.

Tartar: 1-50% (chemically referred to as potassium bitartrate, a salty sediment that remains in wine barrels or forms a yellowish crust around the teeth).

Free acids: 0.3-0.9% (referring to tartaric acid and malic acid).

Minerals: 0.8-1.7%.

Other substances:

In the flesh inside the grape berry, when fully ripe, the following substances are identified in grapes from sun-drenched regions like Iran, where the sugar content is high:

Water: 70-80%.

Fermentable sugar: 17-24% (glucose and fructose).

Potassium bitartrate: 0.5-0.7%.

Free acids: 0.3-0.45% (tartaric acid, malic acid, etc.)

Nitrogen compounds, minerals, fats, and volatile oils (highly variable and low in quantity).

Additionally, there is approximately 0.05 milligrams of arsenic per 100 cubic centimeters of grape water.

In every 100 grams of edible part of raw grapes (grape berries), the following substances are present:

Water: 75-80%.

Protein: 1.3%.

Carbohydrates: 15-22% (depending on the type).

Calcium: 12 milligrams.

Phosphorus: 20 milligrams.

Iron: 0.4 milligrams.

Sodium: 3 milligrams.

Potassium: 173 milligrams.

Vitamin A: 100 international units.

Thiamine: 0.05 milligrams.

Riboflavin: 0.03 milligrams.

Niacin: 0.3 milligrams.

Vitamin C: 4 milligrams.

The following substances have been identified in the grape seeds:

Tannin: 1.6-0.5%.

Tartar: 0.3-0.9%.

Free acids: 1.9-0.2%.

Minerals: 0.4%.

In the grape seeds or kernels, there is tannin and a small amount of extractable oil with a yellowish-green color.

In the grape leaves, various substances have been identified, including sucrose, glucose, inositol, quercetin, tin, courserin, carotene, organic acids, and tartaric acid. In unripe grapes, approximately 3% of organic acids, including oxalic acid, malic acid, tartaric acid, and citric acid, have been identified, as well as a small amount of sugar, around 1%.

Specifications

The wild grapevine is a climbing tree that reaches 10-15 meters above neighboring forest trees. Its leaves are palmate with five leaflets, each with serrated edges in some varieties and smooth or sparsely serrated edges in others. The upper surface of the leaves is smooth, light green or dark green, while the lower surface is usually uneven, rough, and matte green. Its flowers are clustered, tall, and its fruits are round clusters of black or green berries. The seeds are small, oval, and pear-shaped with a short tip.

Propagation of the wild grapevine, like many other plants, can generally be done through seed planting, hardwood cuttings, and grafting. However, the most common method is through stem cuttings and hardwood grafting, which not only saves time but also ensures that the new tree will have the same type of hair as the cutting. The wild grapevine tree can be found in all northern forests of Iran from Gorgan to Arasbaran, as well as in the cold forests of Sardasht in Kurdistan and Sefiddasht in Lorestan. Various varieties of this tree are also cultivated in all tropical and temperate regions of the country. According to agricultural experts in Iran, more than 300 different grape varieties are planted in various regions of Iran.

19. Green Plum[1]

Other names:

Halehoolah, Shal-e-holoo, Alcheh.

Scientific name:

Prunus divaricata Leeb.

Medicinal forms:

Fruit, leaves, flowers, gum.

Therapeutic properties and usage:

In terms of nature, sweet varieties of its fruit are cold and moist while the sour type is colder. Its leaves are cold and dry and astringent.

Its fruit has laxative properties. If eaten before meals, it is useful for warm headaches and bilious fevers. It quenches thirst, reduces heart heat, and relieves itching of the body. It is also a mild cholagogue and soothes disorders caused by bile, especially the slightly sour and sweet type. Its mixture with other suitable medicines is prescribed for stopping white vaginal secretions. It is useful for regulating menstruation in cases of irregularity.

---

1. Aloocheh

Characteristics:

It is a shrub with no thorns or slightly thorny. Its height reaches up to 3 meters. It grows in the forests of northern Iran and bears small egg-shaped fruits with a diameter of 2-3 centimeters. After ripening, the fruit turns yellow and red and tends towards purple. Its taste is sour and sweet.[1]

---

[1]. Prunus divaricata Ledeb. sub caspica Kov & Ekim is a species that grows in the forests of northern Iran and in the deciduous forests from Gorgan to Tavalish. It is a tree that can reach up to 5 meters in height. Its fruit is round and orange with a red tint, and when ripe, it tastes sweet like an unripe tomato. Prunus divaricata Ledeb. sub divaricata is also known as "aloochch" and can be found not only in northern forests but also in steppe regions of the country, such as Kermanshah in the foothills of Mount Parou and Bisotoun, Hamedan, Nahavand, Sepid Dasht Lorestān, and in the Ghich Gardens of Shiraz Castle and Tochal around Tehran.

20. Guava

Other names:

Guava.[1]

Latin name:

Guava and Common Guava.

Scientific name:

Psidium guajava L, and it belongs to the family Myrtaceae.

Medicinal parts:

Fruit, stem bark, and root.

Therapeutic properties and usage:

All parts of the plant (including young and unripe fruits) have an astringent property.

---

1. It is cultivated in Iran, and in northern Iran, it is known by its foreign name, guava, and in the south, it is mistakenly called "Zaytoon" (olive).

Throughout the Far East, from China to the Philippines, the boiled leaves or a mixture of boiled leaves, stem bark, and root bark are consumed as an antidiarrheal. In the Philippines, the boiled bark or dried bark is used to treat stomach pain, and when a more concentrated preparation is made for external use, it is used to relieve skin discomfort, scabies, and wounds.

The cooked leaves are used to make external dressings, and the plant leaves are used as a mild antibiotic against Staphylococcus. Chewed and mashed leaves that have been contaminated with saliva are useful for stopping bleeding and promoting wound healing. The leaves can be used as tea and consumed like tea. Boiled leaves and bark are used as a tonic; they are also given to newborns.

The concentrated juice of the fruit is beneficial for diabetes. The dried ripe fruit is consumed to treat bloody diarrhea. The fruit of guava is a chest softener, a tonic, and mildly laxative. Guava fruit is rich in vitamin B. This plant is also an insect repellent.

Composition:

Guava fruit contains terpenoid essential oil, volatile oil, tannins, fixed oil, and eugenol. Laboratory studies conducted in India have shown the presence of essential oils and eugenol in the plant leaves. Recent chemical studies in India have revealed that the amount of plant essential oil obtained from Allahabad, India is 31%, which includes d-limonene.

The fruit of guava contains guava pectin, which consists of D-galacturonic acid, L-arabinose, and D-galactose. Ellagic acid is found in the stem bark of the plant. Beta-sitosterol, maslinic acid or crategolic acid, guajavalic acid, and another unidentified acid are present in the leaves.

In every 100 grams of ripe guava fruit, the following substances are present:

- Water: 82%.
- Protein: 8 grams.
- Fat: 6 grams.
- Carbohydrates: 15%.
- Ash: 6.
- Calcium: 23 milligrams.
- Phosphorus: 42 milligrams.
- Iron: 9 milligrams.
- Sodium: 4 milligrams.
- Potassium: 289 milligrams.
- Vitamin A: 280 International Units.
- Thiamine: 0.05 milligrams.
- Riboflavin: 0.05 milligrams.
- Niacin: 1.2 milligrams.
- Vitamin C (ascorbic acid): 242 milligrams.

Description:

Guava is an evergreen shrub with leaves that are smooth or covered with a light fuzz but not cracked. Its flowers are highly fragrant.

The fruit, known as "Baie" or "Meaty Berry," contains seeds embedded in its flesh, similar to grape seeds. The fruit has dimensions resembling small olives or pomegranates. In Greek, it is called "Psidium," which means pomegranate. It has a crown-like structure on top of the fruit, similar to a pomegranate, which remains until the end. The fruit's color can be red or yellow.

Guava is sweet and edible, consumed raw or cooked as jams and jellies. It is native to the Americas, particularly the tropical and subtropical regions, and is grown commercially in Brazil and Central America. It has been introduced to Iran and is cultivated in the north and south of the country.

21. Hawthorn

Other Names:

maytree, thornapple, white thorn tree, hawthorn, kamarkajil, markh, kutkuti.

Other Latin names:

Maytree, Thornapple, White thorn tree, Haw thorn.

Scientific name:

Crataegus, from the Rosaceae family.

Medicinal Properties and Usage:

Hawthorn is considered cold and dry in nature, and the bark of the tree is used as a fever reducer. In general, a decoction of hawthorn flowers or dried hawthorn flowers in the amount of 5-8 grams per day is beneficial for heart weakness, angina, edema, aortic disorders, and neurological disorders such as anxiety, insomnia, dizziness, tinnitus, and similar conditions.

In China, an extract is prepared from the dried root bark of the C.monogynus species, which has the property of opening and dilating heart arteries.

In Korea, the fruit of the C.Pinnatifidus species is used to relieve gastrointestinal discomfort and diarrhea. It is noted that in China, people commonly consume hawthorn as a fruit, so it cannot have severe adverse physiological effects on the body's system. In general, hawthorn fruit is considered a mild laxative, stomach tonic, heart tonic, and artery dilator. Some believe that hawthorn fruit charcoal is very beneficial and highly effective in treating indigestion, especially for stopping diarrhea. In India, a watery extract of hawthorn fruit is consumed as a heart tonic to strengthen the heart and treat organic and functional heart diseases.

Hawthorn is prescribed for dyspnea[1] (shortness of breath) caused by cardiac lesions, myocardial hypertrophy (enlargement of the heart), and heart weakness. In France, a tablespoon of hawthorn flowers is steeped in a cup of boiling water, and 2-3 cups of it are consumed daily as an antispasmodic and to alleviate insomnia and discomfort during menopause.

Composition:

The following substances have been identified in the Crataegus oxyacantha species: oxalic acid, glycosides, and a bitter compound called crataegin, which is similar to scolopin. The extract of young green hawthorn branches acts as a respiratory center depressant and has a toxic effect on the hearts of

---

1. The fruit is burned to produce charcoal.

mammals. Fresh hawthorn fruit contains citric acid, tartaric acid, cratagus acid, pectin, oil, fatty acids, glucose, fructose, and its kernel contains amygdalin and emulsin. Its flowers contain essential oils, as well as trimethylamine, aminocoumarin, and coumarins. Another report states that the active compound in hawthorn of the Coxyacantha species is a lactone called cratagoside, which acts as a cardiac stimulant, opening and dilating the coronary arteries. Therefore, it is a cardiac medicine. Flavonoids have been found more in its leaves than in its fruit.[1]

Characteristics:

Hawthorn is a shrub with short thorns, reaching a height of about 7 meters. Its young branches are hairy and then become smooth and white to brownish. Its leaves are ovate with serrations and usually deeply divided into several lobes at the tip, resembling parsley leaves with palmate divisions. Its fruit is round, yellowish to reddish, with a diameter of 1.5-2 centimeters and contains several seeds. It has a sour and sweet taste.

1. This species is distributed in the Middle East, from Syria, Lebanon, and Iraq to Anatolia, Iran, and Turkestan. In Iran, it is found in the Zagros Mountains, Hamadan, Arak, western Lorestan, the heights of Karaj Valley, Zanjan, Kuhchin in Siah Bisheh, and Chalus.

---

1. Dyspnea caused by cardiac lesions.

2. Crataegus atrosanguinea Pojark is a short tree or shrub, reaching a height of 12-10 meters. Its fruit is red with white spots and has two seeds. This tree is found in Armenia, Iran, and Iraq. In Iran, it is scattered in Arasbaran, Kurdistan, Torbat-e Heydarieh, Karaj, and Qom.
3. Crataegus cameyeri Polark is a small tree or shrub, reaching a height of up to 4 meters. Its fruit is round and red, with a diameter of 2-1 centimeters, and its stalk is 10-3 centimeters long. This shrub is distributed in Turkey, Armenia, and in Iran, from the Alborz and Zagros Mountains, from Darband-e Roodbar, Chalus, Kalardasht, Dasht-e Nazir, Pol Zangoleh, Arasbaran, to the heights of Bakhtiari, Lorestan, and the mountains of Baraz Kerman.
4. Crataegus microphylla is a thorny shrub. Its small egg-shaped fruit measures 16-9 mm in length. It is found in the northern forests from Ramian to Rudbar, Astara, Ardabil, as well as in western Iran in Mahidasht, Bakhtaran, and in Lorestan in Dorud. It is also distributed in Khorasan.
5. Crataegus monogyna Jacq is a tree with central thorns measuring 2-1 centimeters in length. Its flowers are white or pink, and its fruit is almost round and red, with a diameter of about 1 centimeter. This species, which has two types in Iran, is found in the Zagros Mountains, Isfahan, Sepiddasht in Lorestan, and on the road from Qom to Tehran at an altitude of 1000 meters.

6. Crataegus monogyna Jac var rubroplena is a beautiful tree planted in gardens. It has pink blossoms in spring.
7. Crataegus pentagna Waldst & Kit. is a tree that reaches a height of 8 meters, with few and short thorns. Its fruit is black or dark purple and spherical, with a diameter of 1 centimeter and several varieties. It is distributed in the northern jungles of Iran from Gorgan and Ramian to Astara.
8. Crataegus persica Pojark is a tree reaching a height of 6-5 meters. Its fruit is egg-shaped and red, measuring 1.5-1 centimeter in length. This tree is seen in the Bakhtiari heights.
9. Crataegus pontica Koch is distributed in Bakhtiari and the mountains of Baraz Kerman. It is also seen in the Chalus Valley at an altitude of 900 meters above sea level. It is a 10-meter tree without thorns, and its fruit is almost round and yellowish, with a diameter of 12-8 millimeters.
10. Crataegus sudoambigua Ajark is a thornless tree. Its fruit is egg-shaped and dark purple. It is seen in the mountains of Hazar Masjed in Khorasan and in the foothills of the Alborz Mountains in Shirpala.
11. Crataegus pennatifidus Bge is a thornless tree. Its immature fruit has a cork-like texture and turns red and smooth after ripening. This tree is found in Karaj.

To propagate hawthorn, its seeds are sown in sandy soil before winter, and after planting, they are transferred to the orchard location in the second and third year seedling nurseries. To obtain ornamental varieties, grafting is done on wild hawthorn rootstocks.

22. Kiwi

Latin name:

Kiwi fruit.

Scientific name:

Actinidia belongs to the Dilleniaceae family, genus Actinidia.

Medicinal forms:

Fruit.

Medicinal Properties and Usage:

In China and Japan, a syrup called "Polygamel" is made from the fruit of the A.polygama variety, which is consumed to strengthen the heart and is believed to have diuretic properties. Dried mature kiwi fruit is used for treating rheumatism and colic. In Korea, the fruit and leaves of the A. arguta variety are used as antipyretics, thirst relievers, and insecticides. In China, the sour fruit of the A. chinensis variety is consumed as an astringent and to quench thirst. It is also a rich source of vitamin C for alleviating vitamin C deficiency symptoms. The plant's leaves and branches are used as insecticides, and boiling them creates an insecticide solution.

In China, the fruit of the A. rufa variety is used to treat anal fistula.

Composition:

The fruit of the A.polygama variety contains tartaric acid, and the fruit of the A.chinensis variety is rich in vitamin C.

Specifications:

Kiwi is a climbing plant, and some of its species have upward growth. Its leaves are relatively round and covered with fuzz. The fruit is greenish and about the size of an egg or a large plum. It is edible, with a more tart taste when unripe.

Kiwi is a plant with four well-known species.

- Acticidia polygama (sieb. & zucc.) piacch. ex Maxim.
- Actinidia (sieb. & zucc.) piacch. ex Maxim Y.
- Actinidia Chinensis plamch.
- Actinidia rufa plamch F.

Out of the four mentioned species, two species, Rufa and Chinensis, have edible fruits. These shrubs have been introduced to Iran and cultivated in Ramsar. They are considered as substitutes for citrus fruits, which are susceptible to frost damage in Ramsar's favorable climate conditions, as these shrubs are cold-resistant. Furthermore, their fruits are a rich source of vitamin C. These seedlings have now grown into trees and have been propagated to other parts of northern Iran, where they have become fruitful and their fruits have entered the market.

23. Mango

Other Names:

Entaj, Anb and Naghzak.

Latin Name:

Mango.[1]

Scientific name:

Mangifera indica.

Family:

Anacardiaceae.

Medicinal Forms:

Fruit, tree bark, leaves, root bark, kernel seed, flower.

---

1. The species referred to in this section is the Indian mango, known as Manguier des Indes.

Therapeutic Properties and Usage:

The bark of the tree is astringent and is used in cases of dysentery, rheumatism, and uterine bleeding.

Mango gum is considered a substitute for Arabic gum in terms of medicinal properties. It is used to treat cracked heels and is also used as an anti-syphilis and scabies medication.

Extracts from the leaves, stem bark, and unripe fruit of mango have limited antibacterial properties against Micrococcus pyogenes var. aureus. Ripe mango fruit has antifungal properties.[1]

Usually, boiled leaves, stem bark, fruit kernel, and gum are used in medicine. The kernel is astringent, free from toxic substances, and contains some amino acids. The powdered kernel is used as an anthelmintic and in cases of hemorrhoids. The ripe fruit relieves thirst and improves blood circulation. The fruit peel has strengthening and toning properties. The dried and cut pieces of unripe mango fruit are used in cases of septicemia.

Mango leaves are soaked and consumed as a cooling drink, similar to herbal tea. They are also used for reducing fever and relieving cold symptoms by applying compresses, taking baths, or using wet compresses.

---

1. Scabies is a contagious skin disease caused by the Sarcoptes scabiei mite. Septicemia is a condition where a large number of pathogenic microorganisms in the blood of a person cause illness.

Burnt and charcoalized mango leaves are used to make candles for repelling mosquitoes, and the powder is used to stop bleeding. In the Philippines, the root bark is used as a diuretic, astringent, and anti-rheumatic agent. In cases of rheumatism, the powdered root bark is boiled in large quantities, and the body and painful rheumatic areas are bathed with it. It is also used for personal hygiene to prevent or stop vaginal discharge.

The kernel is used to treat colds, severe coughs, and hard stools. It is also used to treat hemorrhoids and stop uterine bleeding outside the menstrual period. It is eaten after being soaked and has anti-diarrheal and anthelmintic properties. The gum from the kernel is used to heal mouth ulcers, as well as for its anti-syphilis and anti-diarrheal effects. Mixing it with oil and lemon juice is very effective in relieving skin discomfort.

Sweetness:

Raw and unripe mango fruit is considered cold, dry, and phlegm- and bile-producing, while ripe mango fruit is warm and dry. It is highly nutritious and beneficial for respiratory organs, lungs, stomach, intestines, kidneys, and bladder. It strengthens the bladder and sexual power, brightens the complexion, freshens the breath, and relieves cold headaches, shortness of breath, cough, hemorrhoids, thirst, weakness, fatigue, and body lethargy. It increases urine secretion and, although it has astringent properties, it also provides relief. Mango is harmful for those with warm temperament, especially when the stomach is empty. Therefore, it should be consumed with vinegar or cooled yogurt.

Mango is claimed to have heavy digestion and cause diseases such as jaundice, itching, scabies, and abscesses. To alleviate bloating, it is suggested to consume mango with ginger or sprinkle salt on it, or mix ginger and salt and eat it.

It weakens the liver, so it should be consumed with barberry syrup and sycamore fig to strengthen the liver. It is harmful to gums and teeth and dilutes sperm. To gain weight and enhance sexual potency, it is recommended to consume fresh milk with mango.

Fresh sour mango relieves bile and stimulates appetite, but it is harmful for phlegmatic and jaundiced temperaments. The kernel of mango is used to relieve asthma.

Mango sap is very hot and irritates the skin, and it has an unpleasant pungent odor similar to the smell of benne (a type of wild pistachio). To alleviate discomfort, it should be applied to the area of the skin where mango sap has been spilled.

Mango blossom and mango kernel are very cold and dry. They completely stop diarrhea and act as a sperm dryness and binding agent, especially if the kernel has been slightly roasted. If the fresh blossom is dried and consumed daily in about 4-3 grams with 12-10 grams of sugar, it prevents excessive sperm flow and rapid ejaculation. If the leaf and blossom are ground, soaked in water, and mixed, gargling with this water strengthens the teeth and gums.

Sprinkling wood ash and leaf powder of mango is beneficial for preventing bleeding, and smoking dried leaf or dried skin of mango in a pipe or cigarette is beneficial for expelling kidney winds. Rubbing the water of young mango leaves and rubbing oil obtained from raw mango skin exposed to sunlight is beneficial for hair growth, darkening, and preventing hair loss. In some cases, confectioners use mango kernel instead of sweet almond kernel. Generally, before eating ripe mango fruit, its roots should be cut off, and in addition, the part with sap should be removed and then consumed. The more mature the fruit, the less sap it contains, which is skin-irritating, damaging, and extremely hot.

Composition:

Mango is reported to contain mangiferin, frain, manginin, and a yellow pigment called puree or yelloday. It contains benzoic acid and about 10% tannin. Its kernel is a rich source of fats, carbon hydrates, tannin, and gallic acid. The fixed oil present in it includes oleodistarin. Calcium, magnesium, and phosphorus are found in its ash. Chemical analysis of its kernel shows the absence of alkaloids, glycosides, saponins, and essential oils. Mango flowers contain about 0.04% essential oil and are separated from the skin of the mango tree.

Mango root contains mangiferin, frain, frideline, and betasitosterol. In every 100 grams of raw mango fruit, the following substances are present: water 81 grams, carbohydrates 16.8 grams, calcium 10 grams, phosphorus 13 milligrams, iron

0.4 milligrams, sodium 7 milligrams, potassium 189 milligrams, vitamin A 4800 International Units, thiamine 0.05 milligrams, riboflavin 0.05 milligrams, niacin 1.1 milligrams, and vitamin C 35 milligrams.

Specifications:

It is a large tree that can reach up to 24 meters in height. Its leaves are lanceolate, and its flowers are clustered at the end of the flowering branches.

Its fruit is egg-shaped, edible, and sweet. The sweet flesh is located in the center of the fruit, which is a large seed.

This tree is native to India, Malaysia, and Malta, and is now cultivated in other regions of Asia, such as Java. In Iran, it is grown in the south.

24. Medlar

Other names:

Head, Zar and Tarsheh Sar, Kons, Talas, Gur, Kenduz, Kanas, Kojor, Kendes, Telka, Zoroore Kanas Tabari, Nidania and Mashmala.

Latin name:

Medlar and Medlar tree.

Scientific name:

Mespilus germanica L from the family Rosaceae.

Medicinal properties:

Fruit and leaves.

Therapeutic Properties and Usage:

Medlar is cool and dry in nature and has a significant amount of tannin which makes it astringent and strengthening for the stomach. It reduces intestinal swelling and is very effective in treating simple diarrhea. If unripe, it is more astringent and is useful in preventing bleeding.

Boiled medlar leaves, where 50 grams of leaves are boiled in 1000 grams of water, are used as a gargle to relieve throat and pharyngeal discomfort.[1]

Composition:

The skin, leaves, and fruit of medlar contain a significant amount of tannin. In addition, the fruit contains pulp, some sugar, and about 1% organic acids such as malic acid and citric acid.

Specifications:

Medlar is a small tree used for consumption and medicinal purposes. Its fruit is round and sometimes pear-shaped with brownish-orange skin and white flesh. The wood of the tree is hard and light brown in color.

---

1. Medlar syrup: Remove the skin and seeds from about 200 grams of unripe medlar fruit and cut the flesh into small pieces. Boil in one liter of water for about 15-20 minutes, then add about 50 grams of fresh medlar leaves and simmer for 4-5 hours. Add sugar to make a thick syrup. This syrup is given to children in the evening to relieve diarrhea and stomach cramps and is very useful.1- The wood of medlar is used by villagers to make walking sticks and handcrafted items.

25. Nectarine Fruit

Other names:

Shalil, Indian Cucumber, Mahal.

Latin names:

Nectarine, smooth, and peach.

Scientific name:

Prunus persica nucipersica Boekh.ale pli.

Medicinal forms:

The flower, leaf, and kernel of the fruit are used for medicinal purposes.

Therapeutic properties and usage:

Similar to peaches, in traditional medicine, various parts of the peach tree are used, including the kernel, flower, leaf, and even the root bark. The kernel of the peach is a laxative, purifies the blood, has antispasmodic properties, soothes coughs, and is beneficial for rheumatism. It can stop bleeding, especially uterine bleeding. Additionally, it is prescribed for blood pressure reduction, blood-related diseases, pregnant women's conditions, stomach pain, and anemia. The flower of the peach is a mild laxative and diuretic, beneficial for edema and reducing urinary secretion. Approximately 20 grams of dried peach flowers are used with one liter of milk as a laxative for adults, and 43 grams of flowers are used with one liter of milk or boiled water for children.[1]

In China, young flowering branches and unripe peach fruits are eaten in cases of irregularities and discomforts of women's menstrual periods and bleeding and hernia with other substances. Its decoction is used as a wash for itching and the remaining pulp is dried and made into a round shape and mixed with vinegar and sprinkled on the abscesses.

Internally, it is beneficial for urinary tract diseases, kidney stones, bladder swelling, and chronic cough. The fruit of the peach stimulates the stomach and is useful for relieving inflammation and itching of the skin. It is rich in vitamins C and A, and also has anti-ascorbid properties.

Peach is considered cold and moist in nature. It acts as a mild laxative and relieves thirst. It reduces blood and bile agitation, cools the brain, moisturizes the body's temperament, and reduces

---

[1]. It should be noted that excessive and prolonged consumption of peach kernels, due to the presence of amygdalin and cyanogenic acid released during digestion, can be dangerous and poisonous. Therefore, the consumption of peach kernel should be done under the supervision and recommendation of a physician, considering the appropriate quantity and method.

pure bilious and sanguineous fevers. It is also beneficial for treating bad breath.

Peach is a tonic for individuals with hot temperaments and moist conditions, and it increases appetite. If consumed with water, approximately 200 grams of peach mixed with sugar or tangerine peel can act as a laxative for bile and be useful for relieving burned and hot temperaments.

Peach is harmful for individuals with cold temperaments and phlegmatic conditions, as well as for the nerves. It quickly becomes infected and can cause chronic fevers. In such cases, it should be consumed with ginger honey or ginger jam. Cardi peach is difficult to digest, astringent, and flatulent, especially when consumed raw or dried. The leaves of the cardi peach are also slow to digest.

Consuming 60 grams of water from peach leaves and blossoms alone or with sugar is highly effective in killing stomach and intestinal worms.

Peach kernel oil is beneficial for earaches, earwax blockages, and opening clogged ear canals. If the peach kernel is burned and the kernel is extracted,[1] it can be applied to wounds on children's bodies and behind their ears, which is very effective. Some Hakims prefer fresh peach blossoms mixed with peach blossom

---

1. Glucoside amygdalin releases cyanide under the influence of the enzyme emulsin in a moist environment. Therefore, peach kernel is toxic, and excessive consumption can lead to poisoning. In some cases where it is necessary for certain discomforts, a small amount of peach kernel is prescribed for treatment, but caution must be exercised and it should be done under the supervision of a physician.

syrup. This syrup[1] has the smell of bitter almonds, it is a laxative, and it is very common for children, the amount of this syrup is 30 to 60 grams, and in stomach anthelmintic decoctions, this syrup is also added to make it sweeter and facilitate the expulsion of the animal.

Ingredients:

Similar to peaches, various parts of the nectarine tree are used in traditional medicine, including the pit, flower, leaf, and even the root bark. The nectarine pit acts as a laxative, purifies the blood, possesses anticonvulsant properties, soothes coughs, and is beneficial for rheumatism. It can also stop bleeding, especially uterine bleeding. Additionally, it is useful for reducing blood pressure, blood disorders, pregnancy conditions, and pain.

Composition:

In every 100 grams of edible raw nectarine fruit, the following substances are present: 81% water, 17% carbohydrates, 4 milligrams of calcium, 24 milligrams of phosphorus, 0.5 milligrams of iron, 6 milligrams of sodium, 294 milligrams of

---

1. One unit of dried peach blossom and a sufficient amount of sugar should be steeped in boiling water for 6 hours, Crush with gentle pressure, let it settle, remove the clear liquid from the bottom, and add sugar in a ratio of 10 to 18.

potassium, 1650 international units of vitamin A, and 13 milligrams of vitamin C.

Specifications:

Another species of peach is called nectarine. It has not been seen in Iran in its native and wild form, and its propagation is done through grafting.

26. Orange

Latin Name:

Orange and Common orange.

Scientific name:

Citrus sinensis L. osbeck.

Family:

Rutaceae.

Medicinal Forms:

Fruit, peel, seeds, flowers, leaves.

Therapeutic Properties and Usage:

Orange peel and juice are invigorating, stomachic, aromatic, carminative, antiseptic, diuretic, and chest softeners. Consuming boiled orange peel is beneficial for calming cough, colds, and indigestion. Crushed orange peel serves as an ointment for eczema and skin irritations. Boiled orange leaves, like other citrus leaves, are beneficial for washing and reducing swelling and pain.

Orange is generally antispasmodic and soothing.

Orange essence has disinfectant properties and is derived from its peel. Since it spoils quickly, it should always be consumed fresh, and if stored, it should be kept in a dark and cool place.

In India, it is believed that oranges purify the blood, relieve thirst, and stimulate appetite. Orange juice is beneficial for relieving hepatic discomfort and jaundice-related diarrhea. In China, crushed orange seeds are applied to the face at night to reduce facial blemishes and wrinkles. Orange leaves are used in India and China as a dye, sedative, and for hysteria and hiccup. Orange flower infusion soothes and relaxes in cases of restlessness and heartache, relieves indigestion, and acts as an expectorant for bronchitis. Additionally, orange leaves are chest softeners and are used to treat bronchitis. In the Philippines, orange juice is consumed as a laxative, and a mixture of orange juice and salt is effective against worms and ringworm. Orange essence, when topically applied, is effective for relieving gout and rheumatism pain. Roasted and powdered orange seeds serve as a stimulant.

Composition:

Oranges are a rich source of vitamin C. Its peel contains essential oils, including d-limonene, decyclic aldehyde, linalool, diethyl-terpene-nerol, etc. Neroli is the name of the essential oil obtained from its flowers, and peti green is the name of the essential oil obtained from its leaves and stems.

The leaves contain substances such as l-stachydrine glucoside and hesperidin. In every 100 grams of raw orange, the following substances are present in the peels:

Water: 86 grams.

Protein: 1 gram.

Fat: 2 grams.

Carbohydrates: 12 grams.

Calcium: 41 milligrams.

Phosphorus: 20 milligrams.

Iron: 4 milligrams.

Sodium: 1 milligram.

Potassium: 200 milligrams.

Vitamin A: 200 international units.

Thiamin: 1 milligram.

Riboflavin: 0.04 milligrams.

Vitamin C: 50 milligrams.

In every 100 grams of raw orange peel, the following substances are present:

Water: 72 grams.

Protein: 1.5 milligrams.

Fat: 2 milligrams.

Carbohydrates: 25 grams.

Calcium: 161 milligrams.

Phosphorus: 21 milligrams.

Iron: 8 milligrams.

Sodium: 3 milligrams.

Vitamin A: 420 international units.

Thiamin: 12 milligrams.

Riboflavin: 0.09 milligrams.

Niacin: 9 milligrams.

Vitamin C: 136 milligrams.

Potassium: 212 milligrams.

Specifications:

Orange plant is a small tree with green leaves. Its flowers are fragrant, and its fruits are medium-sized. In some varieties, the peel of the fruit is slightly rough and orange in color, while the flesh is sweet, sour, or mild. It comes in different varieties with yellow, orange, and red colors. Orange trees, and citrus trees in general, cannot tolerate low temperatures and should be cultivated in Mediterranean regions with relatively warm winters. An altitude above 400 meters from sea level is not suitable for these trees, and temperatures below 5-4 degrees Celsius below zero can harm them in the long run. They are grown in northern and southern regions of Iran. Different varieties of oranges are obtained by grafting them onto orange rootstocks derived from seeds. In some cases, orange seeds are also used for propagation to obtain new varieties. Seedling trees bear fruit very late, but their peel becomes thinner, and their taste becomes sweeter.

27. Papaya

Other Names:

Papaya, Melon tree.

Scientific name:

Carica Papaya L, from the family Papayceae.

Medicinal Properties and Usage:

The latex, leaves, fruit, and roots of the plant contain an enzyme that aids in the digestion of albuminoids. Additionally, it possesses antibacterial properties against certain types of bacteria. The latex is usually obtained from unripe papaya fruits and is widely used as a remedy for digestive disorders in Far Eastern countries. Consuming papaya latex has an anthelmintic effect and is effective against roundworm and pinworm infections. It is also noted to be effective against certain types of tumors. In the Far East, papaya latex is used to treat gastric membrane inflammation and enlarged spleen. Externally, papaya latex is used to relieve burns, and it is also considered a beauty treatment for skin blemishes, freckles, eczema, and psoriasis, a skin disease characterized by the presence of red, scaly patches. In Indonesia, it is applied to snakebite sites. In the Philippines, it is used as a first-aid treatment for snakebites, where the upper part of the unripe fruit is pressed onto the site of the snakebite until blood comes out. Fresh papaya root is a skin reddener, but this property diminishes when it dries. The fresh root is used alone or in combination with other drugs to make a mosquito repellent candle, which is useful for treating uterine tumors. Additionally, papaya root is used for hemostasis and as a diuretic for treating kidney stones. In Indonesia, the root and seeds of papaya are used as anthelmintics. The decoction of the root is used for diuretic medication to alleviate discomfort in the bladder, urinary tract, and urine secretion.

In the Philippines, boiled papaya root is used to strengthen the stomach and as a tonic. It is also used in the treatment of hemorrhoids. Fresh papaya leaves are used to make ointments, which act as dressings for wound healing, swelling, boils, and cracked skin. They are also used for healing severe wounds. However, excessive consumption of carpain, an alkaloid present in the leaves and seeds, can cause paralysis and numbness in the nervous system, weaken the heart, and can be effective in treating bloody diarrhea (amoebic dysentery).

The most important use of papaya fruit is for making papain syrup, which contains papain. Dried papaya meat is used in China to reduce foot swelling. In the Philippines, ripe papaya fruit is consumed as a laxative and tonic. In India and China, papaya seeds are consumed in the early stages of embryo formation to induce abortion. It is believed to be effective for early-stage abortions, although it is considered risky.

Studies have been conducted on the enzyme properties of papain, which accelerate blood clotting. Two factors have been found in papaya latex: one accelerates clotting, while the other prevents clotting. Papain latex is usually obtained by making superficial scratches on the fruit's surface, similar to scoring a fruit with shallow cuts. The latex is collected after it oozes out and quickly solidifies. To dry it, it is exposed to sunlight or heat. The dried latex becomes brown in color with an unpleasant odor. This type is called raw papain because it contains impurities. To obtain pure papain, the latex is concentrated in an airless environment, mixed with ten times its weight of absolute alcohol, thoroughly stirred, and the precipitate is dried in a vacuum. Then, absolute alcohol is added again, and the precipitate is collected and dried. This process yields purer papain. Papain dissolves in water but not in alcohol. Drinking a decoction of pineapple roots mixed with papaya roots is beneficial for treating kidney stones.

In India and China, papaya seeds are used to control and treat poisonous insect bites. The dosage of pure papain for relieving indigestion ranges from 10 to 40 milligrams, which is consumed as a syrup, tablet, or elixir. In some cases, adults can consume larger amounts, even up to 2 grams per day, under the supervision of a doctor to kill stomach worms. However, it should be noted that it is toxic and dangerous, and overuse should be avoided. The dosage for children aged 8-7 years is half a teaspoon of the plant's sap, mixed with a little water, honey, and castor oil.

In India, the sap of unripe papaya fruit is used for cosmetic purposes to remove wrinkles, creases, and various types of skin blemishes. This sap is an effective vermifuge, especially for eliminating Lumbrici worms. The ripe fruit is used to strengthen the stomach, act as a carminative and diuretic, and the seeds are used as vermifuge and emmenagogue to relieve thirst.

Composition:

Papain, papayin[1], carposid, and caricin are found in papaya. Fresh papaya fruit contains sucrose, invert sugar, papain, malic acid, salts of tartaric acid, and citric acid. Both ripe and unripe fruits are rich in pectin. Carotenoids are present in papaya fruit. Papaya fruit is a rich source of vitamins. Papaya seeds contain a sulfur compound, which is a significant component of papain. The leaves of the papaya tree contain a glucoside, carposide, and an alkaloid, carpaine.[2]

Vitamin C and E are present in papaya leaves. In the roots of papaya, a glycoside similar to sineigrin, possibly similar to carpain, is found. In addition, there is an enzyme similar to myrosin in the root of papaya, and two types of enzymes called papain and chymopapain have been separated from its crystalline form in papaya latex. Other studies have shown that the following substances are present in the leaves, stem, and root of

---

1. Papaine is also present in papaya seeds, as well as in the skin and roots of the tree, although in smaller amounts. The substance of papain is called plant papain, and it has properties similar to papain, which is beneficial in relieving indigestion and loss of appetite.
2. Carpain is a cardiac poison that is not a cardiac glycoside, but at the same time, it is a powerful amoebicidal agent, meaning it has amoebicidal properties.

papaya: enzyme papain, phytoquinazide, malic acid, calcium malate, and chymopapain in fresh latex. Carpain, carpozide, sucrose, glucose, fructose, and citrates are found in the leaves of papaya, and the seeds contain essential oils.

In every 100 grams of raw papaya flesh consumed, the following substances are present: water 88.7 grams, energy 39 kilocalories, protein 6 grams, fat 1 gram, mostly carbohydrates 9 grams, calcium 20 milligrams, phosphorus 16 milligrams, iron 3 milligrams, sodium 3 milligrams, potassium 234 milligrams, vitamin A 1750 international units, thiamine 0.04 milligrams, riboflavin 0.04 milligrams, niacin 3 milligrams, and vitamin C 56 milligrams.

Specifications:

It is a tree with a cylindrical trunk that reaches a height of 5-6 meters. It has two genders, and the male flowers are white to yellowish with a strong odor, while the female flowers are white. Its leaves are large and serrated, branching out in groups of several leaves resembling fig leaves, connected to a long petiole, and the petiole is attached to the stem, with an average of 8 leaves at the end of each petiole.

Its fruit is small, rescmbling a small watermelon, with a length of 20-35 centimeters and a diameter of 8-10 centimeters. Its skin turns orange when ripe. Inside the fruit, there are numerous coffee-colored seeds, similar in size to black seeds or cardamom seeds. Papaya is propagated by planting its seeds, and it should always be planted with a certain ratio of male to female plants. This tree is native to the tropical regions of Latin America but is currently cultivated and grown semi-wild in India, Mauritius, the Antilles, and other regions. It grows in Baluchistan, Iran, and its fruit is consumed by locals, similar to watermelon, and is very delicious.

28. Paper Mulberry

Other Names:

Paper Mulberry – Toot-ul-Waragh.

Scientific Name:

Broussonetia papyrifera, L'Herit ex Vent.

Family:

Moraceae.

Parts Used:

Leaves, Fruit, Root, Bark.

Medicinal Properties and Usage

All parts of the plant have diuretic properties. The soaked leaves are used to stop nosebleeds and can be applied on eczema. They are also beneficial for wounds, snake bites, and insect stings.

The leaves are used as a laxative and astringent, and they are used to treat colds, flu, bloody diarrhea, and skin diseases when boiled. The bark acts as a hemostatic and anti-hemorrhagic, and it is used to treat continuous thirst, dysentery, and excessive menstrual bleeding.[1] The fruit strengthens the stomach, acts as a tonic, and is a good remedy for kidney disorders and sexual weakness.

The root, when cooked with meat, and its soup, is useful for increasing breast milk secretion.

Components:

The leaf sap contains serotinic acid, proteases, amylase, and chymase. Amylase is present in the leaves.

Specifications:

It is a tree native to China and Japan. The leaves show a variety of shapes and high heterophylly. The egg-shaped leaves have sharp tips, serrated edges, and a bluish color. It is a deciduous tree, and its woody base has sweet red fruits resembling small berries, which are often consumed by children. Paper Mulberry is a fast-growing tree with soft wood that has specific uses in shipbuilding. It is cultivated in Iran.

---

1. When bleeding reaches a point where a sanitary pad becomes saturated within an hour

29. Peach

Other names:

Khukh, Shaftalu, Eshtaludar, Holy Pishmalu.

Latin Name:

Peach.

Scientific name:

Prunus persica (L.) Batsch from the Rosaceae family.[1]

Medicinal Forms:

Fruit, Blossom, Leaf, Kernel, Peel, Root.

Medicinal Properties and Usage:

Peach is considered cold and moist in nature. It has laxative properties and relieves thirst. It reduces blood boiling and bile. It is beneficial for cooling the brain, moistening the body's

---

1. In Iranian botanical documents, the common name for peach tree is mentioned as "persica vulgaris," along with other synonymous names.

temperament, reducing pure bilious and bloody fevers, and eliminating bad breath.

In traditional medicine, the kernel, blossom, leaf, and even the root bark of the peach tree are used in the Far East. The kernel acts as a blood purifier, antispasmodic, and cough reliever. It is also useful for rheumatism, particularly uterine bleeding, and it can help reduce blood pressure. It is generally prescribed for blood-related diseases, pregnancy-related conditions in women, abdominal pain, and anemia.[1]

At least seven famous traditional physicians have stated that peach blossoms have laxative and diuretic properties and are beneficial for treating edema and reducing urinary secretions. Approximately 20 grams of dried peach flowers are brewed in 1000 grams of milk as a laxative for adults, and 43 grams of flowers are used in 1000 grams of milk or boiling water for children to consume in a cup.

Stewart believes that the white part inside the root bark of the peach tree is useful for prevention during disease outbreaks. It is effective in treating edema and jaundice and is a useful and effective medicine. It is also calming and acts as an insecticide, similar to its leaves. Young flowering stems and unripe fruits of peach are used in China for irregularities.

---

1. In these cases, apricot kernels are also used. It should be noted that excessive and long-term consumption of peach kernels, due to the presence of amygdalin and cyanogenic acid released from them, can be dangerous and cause poisoning. Therefore, the consumption should be within the permissible limits and according to the advice of a physician.

It is very beneficial for women's menstrual discomfort, bleeding, and hernia when consumed with other ingredients. Its boiled form is used for washing to relieve itching, and the remaining residue is dried and powdered, then mixed with vinegar and applied to abscesses.

The boiled leaves of peach are used externally for skin diseases and internally for urinary tract disorders, kidney stones, bladder swelling, and productive cough. Peach fruit stimulates the stomach, is beneficial for reducing inflammation and itching of the skin, and is rich in vitamin C and A. It also has anti-scar properties. In hot temperaments, it strengthens sexual potency and increases appetite when consumed with water. Taking about 200 grams of peach with sugar or tangerine blossom acts as a laxative for bile and helps eliminate burnt phlegm. Peach is harmful for individuals with cold temperaments or excessive moisture, and it is also detrimental to the nerves. It quickly becomes infected and can cause chronic fevers, so it should be consumed with ginger honey or ginger jam. The raw and dried forms of peach, especially the dried leaves, are difficult to digest. Eating 60 grams of peach leaves and flowers alone or mixed with sugar is highly effective in killing stomach and pumpkin worms. Ibn Ruzwan, a famous traditional medicine scholar, believes that consuming about 0.5 grams of peach blossoms can cause abortion in certain cases. Peach kernel oil is beneficial for earaches, ear infections, opening clogged ear canals, and relieving hemorrhoid pain. If the peach kernel is thrown into a fire until it burns, then the kernel is removed, crushed, and applied to the wounds and abscesses on the bodies and behind the ears of children, it is highly effective. Some scholars prefer fresh peach blossoms for making peach blossom syrup.[1] This syrup has the smell of bitter almonds, it is laxative and it is very common for children. The dosage of this syrup is 30 to 60 grams. Peach syrup is also used in stomach worm remedies to sweeten the mixture and facilitate the expulsion of parasites.

Ingredients:

Half-open peach blossoms contain trifolin. The kernel of the peach pit contains diastase, emulsin, amygdalin glucoside, as well as procyanidin, choline, and acetylcholine. Peach trees contain prunasin heteroside, and the leaves and branches of the peach tree contain amygdin and nitrile. The green and slender branches of the peach tree contain two flavonol glucosides. Further research indicates that peach tree leaves contain lorosaein and small amounts of various sugars. The kernel of the peach pit contains about 30% fixed oil similar to bitter almond oil. Due to certain reasons, the oil from the moist kernel of the

---

[1]. First, this syrup releases cyanhydric acid as amygdalin glucoside in a humid environment under the influence of emulsin diastase. Therefore, the core of the peach kernel is poisonous and eating more than the allowed amount causes poisoning, and in cases where it is necessary for some reasons and for the treatment of a small amount of the core of the peach core, it should be very carefully and under the supervision of a doctor.
Secondly, peach blossom syrup, dry peach blossom, 1 unit and enough sugar, infuse the blossoms in boiling water for 6 hours, filter with pressure, let it settle, remove the clear water and add sugar in the ratio of 10 and 18.

peach pit cannot be extracted. Peaches can be sweet or sour depending on the variety.

In every 100 grams of delicious peach flesh, the following substances are present:

- Approximately 88 grams of water.
- 9 grams of carbohydrates.
- 9 milligrams of calcium.
- 200 milligrams of potassium.
- 0.5 milligrams of iron.
- 1330 international units of vitamin A.
- 7 milligrams of vitamin C.
- 0.02 milligrams of thiamine.
- 0.05 milligrams of riboflavin.
- 1 milligram of niacin.

Additionally, it contains about 1% of free acids such as citric acid, malic acid, tartaric acid, etc. Peach also contains a significant amount of magnesium. Plant Specifications:

It is a tree that reaches a height of 4-5 meters with multiple branches and angled stems. The stem bark is glossy green and tends to turn red in some parts that face the sun. The leaves are lanceolate or ovate with serrated edges. The upper surface of the leaf is smooth and light green, while the lower surface has slightly veined texture. The leaf petiole is glandless and sometimes glandular, measuring about 2 centimeters in length. The flowers appear early and before the leaves unfold. They are solitary, either without a peduncle or with a very short peduncle.

The color of the flowers can be pink, red, or sometimes white. The fruit has a wide variety of shapes but is generally round, light green, or golden, with a portion of it is red in color, and its outer surface is covered with felt-like cracks. The peach pit is oval and has a grooved surface. The peach pit has a hard woody shell and contains a bitter kernel inside. In some varieties, the peach pit adheres to the flesh, while in others, it does not stick to the fruit flesh. Another type of peach has a smooth and crack-free skin. This type also comes in two varieties: one with a pit that sticks to the flesh and another with a pit that does not stick to the flesh. Peach trees are propagated primarily through seed planting, which is usually done immediately after pit extraction.

Alternatively, they can be propagated through grafting, which is typically done during the months of August and September. Seed planting is usually used to obtain rootstocks for grafting or to develop new varieties. However, from a commercial and general agricultural perspective, grafting is the preferred method of propagating peach trees from the desired cultivars, as it ensures that the desired characteristics of the cultivar will be reflected in the tree. Peach grafting is usually performed on a rootstock derived from a sprouted pit, on almond rootstock, especially in calcareous soils and in areas prone to drought, or on apricot rootstock, particularly in calcareous and rocky soils. Finally, it may also be grafted onto plum rootstock, especially in shallow soils.

In terms of origin, some believe that the peach tree originated from China, while many, including the Chinese themselves, believe that the homeland of the peach tree is Iran, as the name "persica" (referring to Persia, the historical name for Iran) is commonly seen in many nomenclatures.

Wild peaches or plums can be found in the forests of northern Iran, and they are also distributed in the forests of northwestern Iran. Cultivated peaches are grown in almost all regions of Iran and around the world.

30. Pear

Other names:

Kamarud, Anjaseh, Shah Miwa Hussein Abassi, Shah Amrood, Amrood.

Latin name:

Pear.

Scientific name:

Pirus communis L. from the Rosaceae family, genus Pyrus.

Medicinal forms:

Fruit, blossom, seed, leaf.

Therapeutic properties and usage:

In terms of temperament, pear is moderately sweet and coarse, leaning towards warmth and moistness. It is generally a tonic, uplifting, astringent, and at the same time, a mild laxative. It freshens the mouth and is overall astringent, soothing, and febrifuge. It strengthens the heart, stomach, and digestion, relieves palpitations, quenches thirst, and alleviates burning sensation in the bladder. It has a mild purgative effect, but it causes constipation after drying and exertion. All parts of the plant, including the leaf and blossom, have a cold and dry nature. The blossom is a heart tonic and stops bleeding and diarrhea. A poultice made from pear blossoms relieves eye swelling. Pear seeds cause restlessness and have an anthelmintic effect. Eating 10 grams of pear seeds kills and expels worms, and its leaves help stop diarrhea. Eating 20 grams of pear leaves stops diarrhea. The round pear leaf is beneficial for drying and healing wounds, and burning the wood and leaves of the pear has properties similar to Thuya. If the pear is fully ripe and fresh, it is less harmful and beneficial for people with warm temperament, but it is not suitable for people with cold temperament and weak stomach, especially if consumed unripe. In such cases, people with a cold temperament should eat ginger and fennel jam.

Sour pear, also known as Chinese pear, is considered cold and dry in nature. It strengthens the stomach and liver, and increases appetite, relieves blood agitation and bile intensity, and alleviates thirst and it stops vomiting and diarrhea. Sour pears are harmful to elderly people and patients suffering from paralysis and colds. They should be eaten with honey, cumin, frankincense, etc., or as a compote and cooked with sugar and honey to eat. Wild pears, whose varieties in Iran are described at the end of this section, are very cold and dry by nature. In terms of properties, it is astringent and if its dry powder is eaten, it stops diarrhea. Pouring its powder on wounds is useful to dry the wound and heal it. It's plain or mountain types are similar in nature and their properties are similar to wild ones. The fruit of wild pears is very small and hard, so to speak, it has small fleshy grains in its flesh that can be felt under the teeth. The number of its eggs is high, and the "Enchuchak" type pear eggs are used.

The infusion of the young leaves of the pear tree, 100 grams of leaves in 1000 grams of boiling water, which is brewed for about half an hour, is used to treat diabetes and as a diuretic and to remove stones in the urinary tract. Danj "Brouj or Anchonchak egg" which is also said to be a guava seed, is slightly warm in nature and moderately dry in terms of its properties, it is useful for softening the chest and throat and tense nerves. It is fattening and plays a role in increasing sexual power and is a diuretic. If they beat it and take its juice in the water, it is a rule to eat it. Eating too much of it is not good for the stomach and sweets should be used for its side effects.

Ingredients:

In its fresh leaves, 9.82% tannin has been determined. In its dry leaves, 0.3-1.3% of ursulic acid is found. In young pear leaves, there is a new phenolic compound known as compound U, whose physiological effects show that it may be similar to arbutin. The presence of glucoside called phloridzin has been identified in the bark of the root and stem of the pear tree. A little amygdalin and about 15% of fixed oil have been reported in pear seeds.

In every 100 grams of domestic cultivated raw pear with skin, the following substances are present on average: 83% water, 14%

carbon hydrates, 0.4% ash, 8 milligrams of calcium, 11 milligrams of phosphorus, 130 milligrams of potassium, 0.3 milligrams of iron, 2 milligrams of sodium, very low vitamin A (20 international units), 4 milligrams of vitamin C, about 1-2% of free organic acids such as malic acid and citric acid, tannins, etc., 0.02 milligrams of thiamine, 0.04 milligrams of riboflavin, 0.1 milligrams of niacin. The type of sugar present in the pear is mostly fructose, which is also known as levulose.

Characteristics:

The cultivated varieties of pears have large, conical-shaped fruits with sweet or sour flesh and are juicy. Inside the fruit, there are seeds that resemble apple and quince seeds but do not have any gloss. The root of the pear tree is vertical and goes deep into the ground in a conical and thick shape. Pear propagation is mainly done through grafting. Pear grafting can be performed on a rootstock obtained from its own seed. In deep soils, when the pear trees resulting from grafting the desired pear variety on the rootstock obtained from seed take a long time to bear fruit, for example, they start bearing fruit from around the twelfth year. However, pear trees resulting from grafting the desired pear variety on the rootstock obtained from a pear graft start bearing fruit from the 5th to 4th year. In dry lands and soils, usually hawthorn (Aubepine) is used as the rootstock for pear grafting. The most common type of grafting is belly grafting, which is usually done in August at a height of 8-10 centimeters above the plant's collar.

For pear grafting, cleft grafting and crown grafting are also used, especially in cases where the diameter of the rootstock exceeds the thickness of a finger.

Pear is a tree that grows in cool and mountainous regions with mild and lush climates, but it is cultivated in various regions of Iran from moist and semi-moist to dry and semi-dry steppes. This tree has various types in Iran, and different wild species grow in different regions of Iran in the foothills of Alborz and Zagros mountains.

Pyrus:

1. Various species of pears are in Iran, such as Pyrus amygdaliformis Vill. It is a hrub that can reach a height of up to 6 meters. Its branches are thorny and have white bark, which becomes smooth as it matures. The leaves are oval with smooth edges or slightly serrated and covered with long, silky hairs. The flowers are small, clustered, and grayish-white in color. The fruit is almost round, yellowish-brown, with a diameter of 2-3 centimeters. It grows wild in southeastern Europe, Eastern Mediterranean countries, Turkey, and western Azerbaijan in Iran.
2. The pear species Pyrus Boileriana Buhse, known by various local names in different regions of Iran, including "Armot," "Kharas Armot," "Amber," "Hamro," "Amrod," "Gal Arbo," "Suti," and "Yaka and Talco," is a tree that reaches a height of 5 meters. It has thorny branches, and its leaves are egg-shaped with rounded or heart-shaped

bases. Its flowers are white, and the triangular sepals inside the flowers are woolly and reddish. Its fruit is small (1.5 centimeters in diameter), either round or slightly pear-shaped, and sits on a 3-centimeter stalk. It is dark red, tending towards black, with white spots on the surface.

3. The pear species Pyrus communis L, known as "Haj" in Persian, can reach a height of 20 meters. Its branches are thorny, and its leaves are egg-shaped with rounded bases and serrated edges. The young leaves are covered with fuzzy and spiderweb-like hairs, which become smooth later on. The upper side of the leaves is glossy green, while the lower side is brighter. The leaf blade is 7-12 centimeters long and 3-1.5 centimeters wide. The flowers are white, with smooth and fuzzy flower stalks measuring 3-2.5 centimeters in length. The fruit is greenish with a slight reddish tinge, small (4-3 centimeters long and 2-1.5 centimeters in diameter).

4. Pyrus glabra. Boiss is known as "Danj Abruj" in traditional medicine. It is a small tree that can reach a height of 6 meters. Its branches are straight and gray, and its leaves are narrow and spear-shaped. The color of the leaves is olive green and matte. Its small flowers are white, and its fruit is light brown and spherical with a diameter of 1.5-2.5 centimeters. Inside the fruit, there are large seeds. It is known as "Anchuchak," "Ghos," "Armide," or "Golabi Gonjeshk." It is found in the western regions of Azerbaijan, as well as in Sardasht, Kurdistan, Lorestan, Bakhtiari, and the slopes of the

Sisakht-Talkh-e-Khosrow Mountains, Arjan Plain, and Arasbaran.
5. Pyrus hyrcana Fedor is a tree that can reach a height of 25 meters. It has thornless branches and a black bark. The fruit is round and brown with a diameter of 3 centimeters and a short stalk. This species grows in Gilan and northern Iran.
6. Pyrus mazanderanica Schonbech-Temesy is a thorny tree. Its young branches are red and smooth, gradually turning gray. Its leaves are oval with rounded bases.

31. Persian melon

Other Names:

Melon.[1]

Scientific Name:

Cucumis melo L.

Family:

Cucurbitaceae.

Parts Used:

Seeds, Shoots, Fruit Pulp, Fruit Rind.

Medicinal Properties and Usage:

---

1. There are different types of melons, including the late-ripening and early-ripening varieties. Both types belong to the same family and species, and they differ in terms of shape, flesh type, color, and taste, but their medicinal properties are similar. Another type is called "Dastanbu," which is referred to as "Shamameh" in some western regions of Iran. Its skin is wrinkled and fragrant, and it is small in size.

The nature of watermelon is considered mild, moist, and sweet, while its warmth and moistness are moderate in terms of temperature and moisture.

It is believed to moisten the throat and is effective for weight gain. It is also beneficial for jaundice and edema. It acts as a diuretic, promotes menstruation, and increases milk secretion. It is useful for expelling kidney stones.

Watermelon shoots contain a bitter substance that acts as an emetic and diaphoretic. In China, it is common to pick watermelon shoots, give them a smell, and store them in Chinese sealed containers. Whenever there is a need for stomach cleansing in cases of severe indigestion or poisoning that requires emesis, this powder is used as an emetic. It is also used to treat jaundice and nasal ulcers. In the case of nasal ulcers, a small amount of it is inhaled into the nose.

The seeds are used to aid digestion and relieve cough. In India and China, the dried fruit pulp is powdered and mixed with other ingredients to be used as an antiemetic and for relieving restlessness.[1]

The round skin of the melon is used for quick cooking of the flesh. It used to be common in Iran to use the round root of melon as a refreshing tonic, which is beneficial for the kidneys. If eaten on an empty stomach, it causes bile fever, and if eaten after a meal, it makes the food sour. The best time to eat it is between

---

1. For this purpose, about 78 grams of round root were used and consumed.

two meals. Applying melon flesh as a poultice is beneficial for relieving eye inflammation, swelling, and pain, as well as severe swellings. Consuming 8 grams of dried round skin of melon is useful for crushing bladder stones, and if thrown into a pot, it speeds up the cooking of the flesh. Consuming 10-5 grams of its root is refreshing.

Melon is warm and moist in nature and relieves liver congestion and increases urine secretion. It cleanses the kidneys and bladder, acts as a laxative, and increases sexual potency. It is highly effective for treating warm cough, chest pain, and tongue roughness, throat fevers, burning sensation, urinary tract inflammation, and healing acute injuries in the male genital tract caused by the passage of bladder stones. It is harmful to the spleen and should be consumed with honey and violet. The recommended dose of its kernel is 20-8 grams. Consuming the skin and kernel together is highly effective for treating eye inflammation caused by cold and snow. It is preferable to leave the kernel and root together in the skin to dry and avoid separating the kernel and cleaning it.

In China, melons with yellow and red flesh are used to treat liver inflammation. In Guatemala, crushed melon kernels are consumed to expel stomach worms. In the Philippines, crushed melon kernels are used to treat cancer and increase menstrual secretions. In India, melon kernels are consumed as a diuretic. In Africa, crushed melon kernels are mixed with porridge made from grains, especially oats, and consumed for abortifacient purposes.

Components:

Mystic, acid salts, galactan phosphate substance, lysine, citrulline, histidine, tryptophan, and cysteine have been reported in melon seeds. In the fruit, it contains orodaz, peptidase, protease, and vitamins B, A, and C are found. The root of the melon contains melanin emetine. The melon seed kernel contains a considerable amount of fixed oil.

In raw melon and cantaloupe fruit, the following nutrients are present per 100 grams of edible sweet flesh:

Water: 91 grams, carbon hydrates: 7.5 grams, calcium: 14 milligrams, potassium: 251 milligrams, phosphorus: 16 milligrams, vitamin A: 3400 International Units, thiamine: 0.4 milligrams, riboflavin: 0.3 milligrams, niacin: 6 milligrams, vitamin C: 33 milligrams. It can be observed that melons and cantaloupes are rich in vitamins B, A, and C.

Specifications:

The melon plant resembles the cucumber plant and is an annual creeping plant. The leaves are wide, rough, serrated, and hairy, and the flowers are yellow. The flowers appear on the first shoots, and the female flowers appear on younger shoots.

32. Persimmon

Latin name:

Kaki and Japanese persimmon.

Scientific name:

Bi, Diospyros toxburghii Carr & Diospyros schi Bunge.

Medicinal properties and usage:

In modern herbal medicine, the sap obtained from unripe persimmon fruit is primarily used. The flowers' calyx, flower petals, and the second part of the flower located beneath the petals are also utilized. In China, persimmon fruit is used to strengthen the stomach, as an astringent and expectorant for the chest, and it is beneficial for soothing coughs. The sap obtained from pressing unripe persimmon fruit is highly effective in lowering high blood pressure. It stops bleeding and reduces swelling and inflammation of hemorrhoids. It acts as a laxative and is an effective remedy for typhoid and typhus. The infusion made from the calyx and flower tails is beneficial for treating severe coughs, difficult breathing, and shortness of breath, and it is also useful for nausea. The flower infusion strengthens the stomach, acts as an antiemetic and antitussive. The bark and wood of the persimmon tree are prescribed as an astringent for excessive secretions and to stop bleeding in wounds and surgeries. The leaf infusion is antitussive and febrifuge. The root is an astringent.

Composition:

Persimmon fruit contains a significant amount of tannin and sucrose, as well as trioxobenzoic acid, trioxobenzoic acid, arabinose, pentosane, lycopene, zeaxanthin, oxidase, and vitamins B, A, and C, and carotene.

The seeds contain mannans, and unripe persimmon fruit contains shibuol, which helps reduce high blood pressure. The active substances are fluoroglucosol and gallic acid. The green leaves beneath the flowers contain crystalline substances, except for the base. Another report indicates the presence of sitosterol in persimmon wood, and in addition, persimmon contains about 0.02% flavonoids and astragalin.

In 100 grams of ripe persimmon, the following components are present: water 78 grams, protein 0.7 grams, carbohydrate 19.7 grams, calcium 6 milligrams, phosphorus 26 milligrams, sodium 6 milligrams, potassium 174 milligrams, manganese 2710 international units, thiamine 0.03 milligrams, riboflavin 0.02 milligrams, niacin 0.10 milligrams, vitamin C 11 milligrams, and dietary energy 77 calories.

Specifications:

The persimmon plant is a short tree reaching a height of 4-5 meters. Its leaves are simple, alternate, ovate, pointed, and without serrations, with a green henna color. Its small flowers are white in clusters with yellow margins or solitary. The fruit is cylindrical, orange in color, and turns dark red when ripe, similar in size to an apple. The flesh of the fruit is soft and bland when unripe, and sweet and refreshing when ripe. The Persimmon tree is propagated by grafting onto the rootstock of the persimmon tree. Persimmons grown in Iran, especially in coastal areas near the Caspian Sea, are usually seedless, but due to the presence of the persimmon tree, their flowers are pollinated, and they become seedy. Persimmon is native to China and Japan and is cultivated and grafted onto persimmon trees in Iran for propagation[1]. The seeds of Persimmon are ground and used as a substitute for coffee in China.

---

1. Kallu (Diospyros lotus) is abundant in the northern forests of Iran.

33. Pineapple

Latin name:

Pineapple.

Scientific name:

Ananas comosus Merr from the family Bromeliaceae.

Medicinal forms:

Fruit, leaves, and roots.

Therapeutic properties and usage:

The extract from pineapple leaves is an anthelmintic and insecticide. The unripe fruit is effective for abortion, and the extract from the fruit is rich in vitamin C and helpful for treating vitamin C deficiency symptoms. In India and China, the ripe fruit is used as a blood purifier and diuretic. The root is often mixed with papaya root to prepare a tea for treating kidney stones. In the Malian peninsula, the extract from semi-ripe pineapple fruit is used as a strong laxative and for abortion. If consumed in small amounts, it acts as an anthelmintic. Pineapple fruit and its extract aid digestion and are a healing remedy for throat discomforts.

The young leaves of the plant reduce fever and are used for treating infectious diseases. In the Philippines, the yellow liquid obtained by soaking the leaves in water is used to facilitate pregnancy, and crushed leaves are mixed with salt for massaging the back and relieving back pain.

Ingredients:

Bromelain has been identified in the plant, and in every 100 grams of the plant, about 0.008 milligrams of arsenic is found. The extract from the fruit contains bromelain, an enzyme that aids digestion. Another study reported that ripe fruit contains free organic acid sugars, a small amount of vanillin, and bromelain enzyme. In every 100 grams of edible ripe fruit, on average, the following substances are present: water (85 grams), protein (4 grams), fat (2%), carbohydrates (13 grams), ash (0.4 grams), calcium (17 milligrams), phosphorus (8 milligrams), iron (5 milligrams), sodium (1 milligram), potassium (146 milligrams), vitamin A (70 international units), thiamine (0.09 milligrams), riboflavin (0.03 milligrams), niacin (0.2 milligrams), and vitamin C (17 milligrams).

Specifications:

This plant is a perennial herbaceous plant, native to the Antilles and tropical America. Its leaves, which grow in groups from the collar of the plant, are long, narrow, pointed, and hard. Often, there are thorns on the edges of the leaves. The flowers are densely clustered in a pineapple-like fruit that is larger than an egg and has a mixture of pinecone-like scales. The fruit grows in large numbers around the stem, previously covered by the flower, and appears as a fleshy mass. At the top of each fruit, a cluster of leaves in the shape of a rosette can be seen. Some varieties of this plant are grown for ornamental purposes, but the primary goal of cultivating pineapples is to produce a widely consumed fruit.[1]

This tropical plant should be grown in moderate and cold regions and takes at least two years to bear fruit. It is propagated through planting the shoots of the plant or the shoots that grow on top of the fruit.

---

1. Pineapple, originally grown in the Antilles, was later introduced to Europe during the 15th century in the greenhouses and vegetable gardens of Versailles, France, and has since been grown in other warm regions of the world.

34. Plum[1]

Other names:

Gojeh Bargehani, Black Plum, Qatre Tala, Bokhara Plum, Ajass, Baraghooq (Yellow Plum), Qalub Al-Dajaj.

Latin name:

Plum and Garden Plum.

Scientific Name:

Prunus domestica L[2] and belongs to the Rosaceae family.

Medicinal forms:

Fruit, leaves, roots, blossoms, gum.

---

1. There are wild species of plums that grow naturally in Iran, known as "Aluche" or "wild plums," as mentioned in traditional medical texts. They are also referred to as "wild plums" or "sour plums."
2. Another species, scientifically known as P. domestica L. var insititia Bailey, is also called "Alu Bakara."

Therapeutic properties and usage:

From a temperamental perspective, sweet varieties of plum are cool and moist, while sour types are generally cooler. Its leaves are cool and dry, with an astringent property. As for the medicinal properties of the fruit, it acts as a laxative. If eaten before meals, it is beneficial for headaches, feverish conditions, and bilious fevers. It alleviates bile-related thirst, heartburn, and body itchiness. It is a mild laxative for bile and soothes disturbances caused by bile, especially the slightly sour and sweet types. In India, Bokhara plums are prescribed as a laxative and cooling agent, mixed with other suitable medicines, to stop white discharges, soften and lubricate the intestines, and regulate menstrual irregularities. Additionally, it is highly effective for strengthening the body after general weaknesses, fractures, and psychological injuries, providing a soothing effect.

Black plum acts as a laxative and if consumed with honey, it helps eliminate potential harm, especially for cold stomachs. Generally, eating plums before meals has a better effect, and it is recommended to allow sufficient time for digestion before starting the meal.

If dried plums are boiled, strained, and consumed with tamarind, honey, or sugar, they have a stronger laxative effect. Red mountain plum or a type of Qaisi plum is commonly boiled until thickened, and from it, round pieces are made (used for making bread called "lavashak-e aloo"), which is consumed in soups by patients or eaten raw.

Wild plums are harmful to the stomach and cause constipation, as they have a strong astringent effect. Applying its blossoms on the head is beneficial for warming headaches. Gargling and rinsing with boiled leaves and roots of plum are useful for tonsillitis and gum strengthening, while consuming it helps expel stomach worms. It is harmful to the brain, so it should be eaten with jujube, and due to its harmful effect on the stomach, it should be eaten with sugar candy, and in individuals with cold temperaments, it should be consumed with Mastagi and honey.

The recommended dosage of plum for its effectiveness is up to 200 grams, and as a substitute for plum in terms of properties, Tamarind can be used. The gum (the sap of the tree trunk) of plum, known as Persian gum, is warmer than Arabic gum and has less constipating effect. It is beneficial for coughs, breaks down kidney stones, and aids in wound healing. Rubbing it on the eyes increases visual acuity, and applying its poultice with vinegar is beneficial for children's skin boils.

Usage methods:

Plums are used to make soup, jam, vinegar, syrup, and various dishes and beverages, each of which possesses some of its properties.[1]

---

[1]. Recommendation: 1) At the beginning of the plum and water diet, plums may cause feelings of bloating, fullness, flatulence, and various other gastrointestinal discomforts. However, after a while, the intestines adjust to these conditions, and these symptoms will be alleviated within

Composition:

The skin of plum contains about 3% tannin. In fresh fruit, it contains malic acid, citric acid, succinic acid, salicylic acid, and approximately 3-4% sucrose and converted sugars, as well as 4-5% carbon hydrates. In dried fruit, there is a high amount of sugar, around 40% converted sugar and 15-18% carbohydrates. The kernel of plum contains a fatty substance and amygdalin, and by distillation, it yields HCN or hydrocyanic acid. For this reason, the kernel of plum is toxic and bitter, and consuming it is dangerous.

In every 100 grams of cooked fresh plum, the following substances are present: water 78-80 grams, protein 5 grams, sugar and other carbohydrates 12-19 grams, calcium 12 milligrams, phosphorus 17 milligrams, iron 5 milligrams, sodium 1 milligram, vitamin A 300 international units, thiamine 0.03 milligrams, riboflavin 0.03 milligrams, niacin 0.5 milligrams, vitamin C 5 milligrams, and potassium 299 milligrams.

Specifications:

The plum tree is a short tree, usually without thorns, reaching a height of 4-5 meters. Its roots do not grow very deep, and its trunk has hard wood with red veins. The crown of the tree is

---

3 to 4 weeks. 2) At the beginning of the regimen, it is advisable to avoid consuming large amounts of plums, and it is better to start with a small amount and gradually increase it. For example, add an additional 30-35 grams per day until your body becomes accustomed to it.

round in some varieties and elongated in others, resembling an egg shape. The stem's skin is smooth, shiny, and covered with delicate and hairy bark.

The leaves are oval or elongated with serrated margins and hairy on both sides. Its flowers have a diameter of 1.5 to 2.5 centimeters, and the flower stalk is smooth or hairy, about 2 centimeters long. The fruit is egg-shaped or round, and it comes in colors such as yellow, purple, and dark red. It has a small egg-shaped pit attached to the fruit.

Plum trees are not suitable for permanently moist and swampy lands that do not have good drainage. Such conditions can suffocate the roots and cause rotting. Therefore, it is preferable to plant plum trees in relatively dry and permeable soil.

Plum propagation is very simple and can be easily done through methods such as seed planting, branch cutting, or grafting. Once the young sapling is obtained and ready to be transferred to the main location, it is planted in the orchard with a distance of usually 7 to 8 meters. Grafting of plum trees is usually done at the rootstock level, near the soil surface.

Different varieties of plum trees grow naturally in the forests of northern Iran, from Bandar Gaz to Gilan, as well as in mountainous regions around Kermanshah in Bisotun, in western Azerbaijan, and in Fars. They are also cultivated and grown in most regions of Iran.

Plums that are consumed fresh come in various varieties, including Reine-Claude or juicy green or golden yellow plum, which is large and round, Goutte dor or golden drop, which is large and egg-shaped, and Mirabelle or small yellow plum with red dots, which is mainly used for compotes and preserves. Another variety is Saint-Antoine, which is a dark blue plum.

35. Pomegranate

Other names:

Roman fruit.

Latin name:

Pomegrenate.

Scientific name:

Punica granatum from the Puniaceae or Granataceae family.

Medicinal forms:

Fruit, flower, leaf, bark, root & seed.

Properties and usage:

In general, pomegranate is cool and astringent and its concentrated juice is even cooler and less astringent than its peel. The peel of pomegranate is very cold and dry and highly astringent. Sour pomegranate scratches the intestines, especially when consumed on an empty stomach, and can cause intestinal inflammation.

Pomegranate flowers are highly astringent, and the bark and root peels are even more astringent than other parts.

Sweet pomegranate is cool and moderately moist, slightly astringent, and produces healthy phlegm. However, it can cause flatulence, so it is not recommended for people with warm temperaments. It is a laxative and increases urine secretion while being a diuretic. It causes thirst. Sweet pomegranate juice, when consumed after meals, is beneficial for purifying the blood, strengthening the liver, treating jaundice and palpitations, relieving chronic dry coughs, clearing the voice, curing stuttering, and brightening the complexion. Overconsumption can be harmful. It spoils food in the stomach and weakens it, causing bloating. In such cases, sour pomegranate should be used to relieve symptoms. Ginger pudding is also recommended for people with cold temperaments. Sweet pomegranate syrup is stronger than its juice in terms of its effects. To avoid these side effects, it is better to consume it with honey.

If the top of a sweet pomegranate is punctured several times and almond or violet oil is poured into it until it is full, then heated over fire until the oil is absorbed, and then squeezed, it can be very effective for relieving chest pain and chronic dry coughs.

If sweet pomegranate juice is mixed with sugar, starch, gum Arabic, and almond oil, and consumed, it has the same effect.

Pomegranate seeds are flatulent and cause gas in the stomach. Burnt pomegranate flowers are useful for healing and drying wounds. If a few unripe pomegranate flower buds (1 or 2 depending on the age and physical strength of the infant) are mixed with some fresh mature leaves of hawthorn (1 or 2 grams) and a little ground white celery (1 or 2 grams) with half a cup of water, and given to infants or slightly older children, it can relieve simple diarrhea that may cause teething and other minor complications. Sweet and sour pomegranates are moderate in terms of being cool and moist. However, very sour pomegranates are very cold and dry, astringent, and increase urine secretion. They soothe stomach heat and boiling blood, but overconsumption can cause ulcers and inflammation in the intestines. They are harmful to people with cold temperaments, weaken liver function, reduce sexual potency, and therefore should be consumed with sweet pomegranate and ginger pudding or similar foods. A mixture of sweet and sour pomegranate juice (500-250 grams) mixed with about 100 grams of sugar and consumed is a laxative for bile and stomach tonic. It is very useful for treating jaundice, stuttering, and reducing mouth ulcers. Its gargle has an antiseptic effect. Sour pomegranate syrup is stronger than its juice in all cases. If the inside of a pomegranate is emptied and filled with red rose oil and heated over low heat, then a few drops are dripped into the ear, it can be very useful for relieving ear pain. The mixture of sweet and sour pomegranate is cool, dry, astringent, and useful for reducing inflammation, excessive thirst, acute fever, nausea, dizziness, relieving pregnant women of discomfort, and treating yellowing of the complexion.

Pomegranate is a fruit that can be consumed in various forms, including the fruit, flower, leaf, bark, root, and seed. The peel of the pomegranate is very cold and dry and highly astringent, while sour pomegranate can cause intestinal inflammation. Sweet pomegranate is cool and moderately moist, slightly astringent, and produces healthy phlegm. It is a laxative and increases urine secretion while being a diuretic. Sweet pomegranate juice is beneficial for purifying the blood, strengthening the liver, treating jaundice and palpitations, relieving chronic dry coughs, clearing the voice, curing stuttering, and brightening the complexion. Overconsumption can be harmful, causing bloating and weakening the stomach.

Sour pomegranate is very cold and dry, astringent, and increases urine secretion. It soothes stomach heat and boiling blood but can cause ulcers and inflammation in the intestines if over consumed. A mixture of sweet and sour pomegranate juice mixed with sugar is a laxative for bile and stomach tonic. Pomegranate seeds are flatulent and cause gas in the stomach.

Pomegranate flowers are highly astringent, while the bark and root peels are even more astringent than other parts. Pomegranate has various medicinal properties, including being an effective remedy for chest pain, chronic dry coughs, wounds, diarrhea, and teething complications in infants. It also has antibacterial properties and can be used as an antiseptic gargle.

Crushed pomegranate seeds mixed with an equal amount of cumin and one-fifth of its weight of celery are effective for relieving bloating and strengthening the stomach. Pomegranate flowers are commonly used in Iran for treating chronic diarrhea and as an astringent gargle. Pomegranate peel and the white flesh inside it are highly astringent, cold, and drying. Ground and dried pomegranate peel is useful for drying simple shanker ulcers. Gargling with boiled pomegranate peel water strengthens the gums and stops bleeding. Eating dried and ground pomegranate peel mixed with warm water is very useful for expelling stomach and intestinal worms.

Pomegranate root bark is even more effective in all the above cases. Boiled pomegranate root is more effective than other parts for treating tapeworms. Gargling with boiled pomegranate root is very effective for relieving toothache pain.

If you sit in boiled pomegranate peel water, it is useful for stopping excessive menstrual bleeding and other conditions where the anus is prolapsed. Pomegranate bark extract is effective as an anthelmintic against tapeworms and hymenolepis dosis. The aqueous extract of pomegranate peel is less effective than vinegar extract. The anthelmintic effect of pomegranate peel and root bark is due to the presence of iso-pelletierine alkaloids. Pomegranate root bark has an anthelmintic effect against trichinella spiralis. In Southeast Asia, pomegranate root bark and stem bark are used as astringents and anthelmintics, especially against tapeworms.

Some believe that the plant also has antibacterial properties. In India, the root bark and stem bark are used as astringents and anthelmintics, especially against tapeworms. The fruit seeds are good for the stomach, and pomegranate juice is good for the heart and stomach and has a cooling effect.

The plant's ingredients include alkaloids such as peltehthein and... Obtained from pomegranate tree bark. Four alkaloids named Pazud, Peltehthein, Rine, and a large amount of tannin are found in the root bark. In the bark of the Betulic tree, there is also Betulinic acid and Ursolic acid, and both types of acid are found in its leaves. In addition to the four mentioned alkaloids, there are three other basic compounds in the pomegranate tree bark. In every hundred grams of the edible part of the juicy red pomegranate, which surrounds the pomegranate seeds, the following materials exist in raw form: 82 grams of water, 0.5 grams of protein, 0.3 grams of fat, 16 grams of carbohydrates, 3 milligrams of calcium, 8 milligrams of phosphorus, 0.3 milligrams of iron, 3 milligrams of sodium, 259 milligrams of potassium, 0.03 milligrams of thiamine, 0.03 milligrams of riboflavin, 4 milligrams of vitamin C, and 0.3 milligrams of niacin.

Specifications:

Pomegranate is a small tree with slightly serrated branches and completely green and shiny leaves. Its flower is red pomegranate with a large number of male organs and one ovary that has multiple rooms. Its fruit is round, its skin is thick and red, and it contains a large number of hard seeds surrounded by a sweet or sour and sweet red transparent glass-like substance. These seeds and the surrounding edible part make up the pomegranate fruit as a fruit. Pomegranate is a semi-tropical plant that has grown in

Iran since ancient times. It exists in the wild in Baluchistan, around the central desert areas, western and northern Iran, and is also cultivated in most semi-tropical regions of Iran. It is also found in Mesopotamia, North Africa, southern Europe, and Spain.

36. Pomelo

Other names:

Citrus Sultan, In English: Pomelo.

Scientific name:

Citrus grandis (L.) Osbeck.[1]

Medicinal forms:

Bark, leaves, flowers.

Medicinal properties and uses:

In India, the sour juice of pomelo is used as a cardiac tonic and coolant. Its leaves are used for epilepsy and coughs with convulsions.

In China, they use the boiled peel, which is bitter and aromatic, as a stomach tonic, detoxifier, and for treating indigestion. Additionally, it is beneficial for nausea, colds, and respiratory infections. It is also added to wash solutions for relieving itching, scabies, and acne. Its seeds are boiled in water with fennel or

---

1. It has synonyms C. decumana L. and C. maxima.

anise and the resulting water is used for treating hernias, bladder pain, and swelling of the reproductive system.

In the Malay Peninsula, boiled pomelo leaves are used for cleaning wounds, and the warm decoction is applied as a compress to reduce pain and swelling. Furthermore, its leaves are placed on migraines and headaches. In India and China, unripe fruits are halved, dried, and consumed as a tonic and anti-hemorrhagic agent.

In the Philippines, they consume the boiled or decocted leaves, flowers, and peel as a sedative for nervous discomforts. Additionally, it is used to prepare scented baths. Mixing the sour juice with the boiled peel of Achyranthes aspera is beneficial for treating and stopping bloody secretions.

Composition:

In terms of chemical composition, it is similar to grapefruit, and it contains naringin. Its peel contains d-limonene, alpha-pinene, linalool, geraniol, etc. The young and green leaves and stems of this species are also used to extract petitgrain oil.

Characteristics:

It is a citrus fruit similar to grapefruit, and in some regions of Iran, it is also called "grapefruit" but with larger size. The tree resembles a grapefruit tree and has thorns.

This species is more commonly found in China and various regions of India, and it is mostly used for medicinal purposes. In Iran, it is found in the northern parts.

37. Quince

Names:

Abroud, Abi, Sefarjal, Ayva, Huwa, Shaghaleh, Toch, Sange.

Latin Name:

Quince.

Scientific Name:

Cydonia oblonga Mill, from the Rosaceae family.

Medicinal Forms:

Fruit, Seeds, Flowers & Leaves.

Therapeutic Properties and Usage:

Quince leaves, buds, and stem bark have an astringent property. The fruit acts as a chest astringent and heart tonic. Quince seeds are used as antipyretics and for reducing simple diarrhea, dysentery, and throat inflammation. The mucilage from the seeds is beneficial for external use on wounds and burns caused by fire.

The taste of the fruit is sweet and moderately warm or slightly hot in nature. There are generally three types of quince: sweet, sour, and sour-sweet (also known as "malas" in Persian). Quince is a joy-inducing, brain and stomach tonic, and diuretic. Eating raw quince is astringent and obstructs the blood vessels. Raw sweet quince is harmful to warm-tempered individuals.

Sour quince is cold and dry in nature. Its sweet variety is stronger in strengthening the stomach. If consumed in excess, it acts as a laxative. Quince extract is beneficial for respiratory distress, phlegm in the chest, strengthening the stomach, increasing urine secretion, and stopping bleeding.

Sour-sweet or malas quince is moderately hot and cold but dry. Its properties are similar to other types and are useful for relieving restlessness, preventing phlegm, and stopping internal bleeding. It is better to consume quince in the form of jam rather than raw. Applying a drop of quince water to the vagina is beneficial for relieving burning and itching in the urinary tract and genital injuries.

It has healing properties, and if it is roasted until it becomes dark in color and consumed, it is highly effective for treating chronic diarrhea, especially when it is filled with chopped walnut and barley instead of walnut seed. The dosage of this remedy is up to 120 grams.

Oil of Quince[1] from a natural perspective, it is cold, moist, and astringent. It is useful for mouth ulcers and tinnitus. Consuming it helps relieve headaches, warm hemorrhages from the chest, liver swelling, chronic diarrhea, intestinal ulcers, and insect bite poison. It also has the same effect when used for purification or injections.

Beech seeds, from a natural perspective, are mostly cold and moist. The saliva from chewing beech seeds is beneficial for throat inflammation, warm and dry coughs, relieving heat, gastric fever, tongue and mouth burns, and dryness of the tongue and mouth.

Massaging beech saliva onto the skin is useful for soothing and healing burns caused by fire, boiling water, and sunburn. Chewing beech seeds helps alleviate toothache, and its brain, when warm in temperament, is beneficial for strengthening sexual potency. It is also beneficial for tuberculosis, respiratory organs, cough, hoarseness, and intestinal bleeding. The dosage of beech seeds is up to 10 grams, and the dosage of its saliva is up to 50 grams. Beech seeds weaken and impair the stomach, so individuals with warm temperaments should consume them with sugar, while those with cold temperaments should consume them with fennel. Beech seeds can be replaced with asparagus seeds.

---

1. To prepare beech oil, first, the beech nuts are fully cooked and compressed, and their water is removed. Then, the remaining oil is boiled with twice the weight of the collected water until the water evaporates, leaving only the oil. Care must be taken not to burn the oil.

Composition:

The beech kernel contains about 1% amygdalin glucoside, and approximately 19-15% fixed oil can be extracted from the kernel. In the sprouts, a glucoside called cyanogenetic is found.

Hydrocyanic acid (HCN) is obtained from the skin and stems of beech.

The outer shell of the beech seed contains about 20% soluble saliva in water, which, when 5-4 grams of it is mixed with water, produces an egg white-like solution. The beech leaves also contain a small amount of amygdalin glucoside.

Further analysis shows that the beech seed or kernel contains several glucosides, mucilaginous substances, pectin, lipids, resins, and vitamin C. The beech leaves contain approximately 11% tannin and also contain rutin flavonoid. Beech seeds do not contain saponins or tannins. The analysis of the fruit's flesh, which is sweet and slightly sour, shows that it contains various substances, including per 100 grams of flesh.

Fruit Composition:

The following components are present in the fruit:

- Water: 83 grams.
- Sugars and carbohydrates: 15 grams.
- Ash: 0.4 grams.
- Calcium: 11 milligrams.

- Phosphorus: 17 milligrams.
- Iron: 0.7 milligrams.
- Potassium: 197 milligrams.
- Vitamin A: Very low, about 40 international units.
- Vitamin C: Approximately 15 milligrams.
- Thiamine: 0.02 milligrams.
- Riboflavin: 0.03 milligrams.
- Niacin: 0.2 milligrams.
- Sodium: 4 milligrams.

Description:

It is a small tree with a stem and trunk that are brownish in color and do not crack. However, when the tree becomes old, pieces of the bark become detached. The leaves are covered with a layer and have a smooth and unwrinkled surface. Its buds are small and covered with fuzz. The flowers are very large, singular, and have five petals, either white or pink. The fruit is yellow, round or pear-shaped, and its surface is often covered with fuzz. Inside the fruit, there are seeds, usually 12 in each compartment. The tree is native to the eastern part of the Earth and central Asia. It grows naturally in the northern forests of Iran at medium altitudes. The trcc is also propagated by grafting, and the desired varieties are grafted onto the rootstock. Grafted seedlings, which have sufficient growth, are usually planted in gardens with 4-5 meters spacing.[1]

---

1. The genus name Cydonia is derived from the city of Sidon in Lebanon, which has been abundant with these trees.

38. Rose Apple

Other Names:

Jambos.

Scientific Name:

Syzygium Jambos (Alston) from the family Myrtaceae.

Parts Used:

Leaves, Fruit, Root & Bark.

Medicinal Properties and Usage:

In traditional medicine, the boiled leaves of the tree are used to treat eye wounds. In India and China, the bark is used as an astringent, and the water-soaked leaves are used as an antipyretic.

All parts of the plant have stimulating and tonic properties and are useful for relieving toothache. In the Malay Peninsula, the powdered leaves of the tree are applied to the body of patients with chickenpox to reduce fever, and a poultice made from this powder is used to relieve itching. In Indonesia, the astringent properties of the fruit seed and bark are used to treat diarrhea, dysentery, influenza-like fevers, and to strengthen male sperm.

Components:

The leaves and fruit of the tree are rich in tannins. Another report states that the leaves and bark of the tree contain jambosine alkaloid and tannins, as well as a type of gum called olerzin.

Specifications:

It is a tree with long, drooping leaves and fragrant fruits with a scent of red flowers. It is native to Eastern India and is cultivated in tropical Asian regions. In Iran, it is grown in the southern region, and its local name is "Jambos."

39. Sour Cherry[1]

Other names:

Albaloo, Alu-ye Boali, Gharasya (Gharasia, Jharasia), Latin name: Sour cherry and wild cherry.

Scientific name:

Cerasus vulgaris Mill from the Rosaceae family.

Medicinal forms:

Tree bark, kernel, fruit & tea.

Therapeutic properties and usage:

In terms of nature, when the fruit is raw, it is slightly cold, dry, and astringent. When it is half-ripe and turns red and sour, it becomes colder and drier. However, when it is fully ripe and becomes juicy and dark red or black in color, it becomes warm and moist.

---

1. Another type of plum is called the bitter plum, which is also known as Rock cherry in English and belongs to the Rosaceae family.

Tea made from the tree bark is bitter, astringent, and useful for fever and gout. The kernel and its core[1] are nerve tonics and useful for paralysis. It is believed that plum relieves thirst, high blood pressure, liver disorders, diarrhea, and upset stomach. It is a warm tonic for the stomach and liver. Its astringent properties are stronger in dried form than fresh.

If the kernel is crushed and taken with 1% of its weight in caraway seeds, it is beneficial for breaking down kidney and bladder stones and healing urinary tract infections and burning sensations. It regulates menstruation.

Tea or decoction: Plum tea is a diuretic. To prepare plum tea, soak it in cold water for 10-15 hours before boiling 3% of it. After straining it, use it as a diuretic.

Plum syrup is prescribed for reducing fever and chronic liver, intestinal, and kidney swelling.

Ingredients:

In plum, the amount of acids is higher in sour ones, especially cyanide acid HCN. The amount of HCN is higher in the plum kernel, which is a substitute for HCN in medicine. There is a small amount of prussic acid in the plum leaf, which is the same

---

1. The pit and kernel of the plum contain HCN or hydrocyanic acid, which can be toxic if consumed in excessive amounts. The presence of amygdalin glucoside, which is a precursor to HCN, makes it poisonous. Therefore, the internal use of this type of plum should be done with extreme caution and under medical supervision.

as cyanide acid, making plum leaf extract a painkiller. In the Mahaleb species, salicylic acid and amygdalin are present.

Characteristics:

The plum is a small tree or shrub with small green leaves that are smaller than those of cherries, and its flowers are white. Its fruit is smaller than cherries, dark brown or black, slightly sour, and juicy. Its kernel is egg-shaped. The plum tree or shrub is found naturally in Iran in the mountains of Karaj, the slopes of Eshtehard, and in Khorramabad, Lorestan. It is also grown in Iranian gardens.

40. Sour Lemon

Other names:

Lemon, Hill lemons.

Latin name:

Citrus limon.

Scientific name:

Citrus limon (L) Burm, from the Rutaceae family.

Medicinal forms:

Fruit, tree bark & fruit peel.

Therapeutic properties and usage:

Lemon is considered to have a cool and moist nature, and some believe it to be cold and dry. It is believed to be beneficial for hot swellings, palpitations, gastric acidity, inflammation of the stomach and liver, relieving restlessness and heartache. However, it is considered harmful for nerve-related issues and cough, as well as for individuals with a cold temperament.

Excessive consumption of lemon on an empty stomach weakens the intestines and can cause heartburn. In India and China, lemon water is used as an antidote for poisoning from consuming poisonous plants of the Euphorbiaceae family.[1]

The lemon peel is bitter and acts as a stomach strengthener and tonic. It is best consumed when fresh. In China, lemon essential oil is used as an antibiotic for treating typhoid meningitis and other bacterial infections, but excessive use can cause memory loss and confusion.

Lemon water gargle is used to reduce swelling and inflammation in the throat and tonsils, and it is also used as a cleansing solution for wound cleaning. Boiled lemon leaves are used externally to relieve pain and swelling. In general, lemon exhibits analgesic, soothing, and antispasmodic properties.

In India, dried lemon peel is used to strengthen the stomach and as a digestive aid. Freshly squeezed lemon juice is consumed and used as a diuretic and cooling agent, as well as for treating diseases caused by vitamin C deficiency. It is beneficial for

---

1. To prepare lemon water, the peel should be completely removed so that the essential oils from the peel do not mix with the lemon water, as this can accelerate its spoilage. The seeds should also be removed beforehand or the pressure should be gentle enough not to crush the seeds, as crushed seeds can make the lemon water bitter. If the peel is crushed along with the flesh inside the lemon, it can also make the water bitter. It is necessary to sterilize and preserve the lemon water because fresh lemon water contains oxidizing yeasts. It is not advisable to use high heat to sterilize lemon water, as the vitamin C content, or even all of it, will be destroyed by high heat. It is better to use hydrogen gas under pressure, which is commonly done in factories. Lemon water loses a significant amount of its vitamin C content when exposed to sunlight during storage, so it should be stored in a dark place, preferably in dark glass containers.

rheumatism, simple diarrhea, and dysentery. In cases of acute joint rheumatism, 150-120 grams of lemon juice mixed with sugar syrup are consumed gradually throughout the day. Freshly squeezed lemon juice acts as a disinfectant, diuretic, and astringent when obtained from pressed fruit. Gargling with lemon juice can be useful and effective in relieving throat inflammation and pain in cases of colds. Applying lemon juice to the skin is beneficial for sunburn and reduces itching.

In India, lemon is used as a morning beverage by mixing two tablespoons of fresh lemon juice with two tablespoons of honey and 30 grams of water, creating an invigorating and beneficial drink. Placing a cut lemon on the forehead can relieve a warm headache. Lemon juice is useful for scratches and wounds. Lemon peel is warm and dry and has detoxifying properties. Lemon zest is usually consumed by mixing 8-4 grams of it with warm water.

Composition:

The essential oil of lemon peel contains compounds such as d-limonene, alpha-pinene, camphene, linalool, and others. Lemon juice contains an effective anti-pneumonia agent. Lemon peel contains a bitter substance, essential oil, and hesperidin.

In every 100 grams of juicy lemon pulp, the following raw materials are present: 90 grams of water, 1.1 grams of protein, 8 grams of carbohydrates, 0.3 grams of ash, 26 milligrams of calcium, 16 milligrams of phosphorus, 0.6 milligrams of iron, 2 milligrams of sodium, and 138 milligrams of potassium.

Lemon contains 20 international units of vitamin A, 0.04 milligrams of thiamine, 0.02 milligrams of riboflavin, 0.1 milligrams of niacin, and 53 milligrams of vitamin C. Various lemon products are available in the market, including lemonade, citric acid, lemon essential oil, and lemon zest.

Specifications:

Lemon is a small tree, about 4-5 meters in height, with branching and angular branches. Sometimes, it has sharp thorns, and its leaves are green with a slight reddish tint. The top of the flower is white with a hint of purple.

The flesh inside the fruit is white to yellowish and thick. The fruit has a thin skin with numerous glands filled with aromatic essence, giving it a penetrating smell. The seeds inside the fruit are yellow and bitter, and the fruit segments range from 6 to 11, filled with very acidic sour juice.

Lemon is grown in hot regions in Europe and Asia, but most of the world's lemons currently come from the Sicily region of Italy and Kallaberg. In Iran, different varieties of lemon are cultivated. Lemon is extensively propagated in northern and southern Iran through budding on bitter orange or lemon rootstock obtained from seed cultivation.

41. Strawberry

Other Names:

Chilk.

Latin Name:

Strawberry.

Scientific name:

Fragaria vesca.

Family:

Rosaceae.

Medicinal forms:

Fruit, leaf & root bark.

Therapeutic properties and usage:

In India, strawberry fruit is used as an astringent and diuretic, and its underground stems are consumed as a substitute for coffee in Kashmir.

Infusions of strawberry leaves are used for urinary tract infections and urinary discomfort. A very pleasant and diuretic infusion can be prepared from a mixture of strawberry leaves, cinnamon, and vanilla, similar to tea, which is refreshing and diuretic. Infusing 30 grams of strawberry root bark in 1000 grams of water is diuretic and helpful for relieving obstructions. This infusion has a beautiful red color. A 5% decoction of underground stems, leaves, or both of strawberry, used as a gargle, is beneficial for relieving allergies externally. A 2-3% decoction of strawberry leaves, used for kidney stones and stopping bloody diarrhea, is also beneficial as a diuretic for continuous thirst. It is recommended to consume one tablespoon in the morning and evening.

Ingredients:

Strawberry leaves contain ellagic acid and the red color of the fruit is due to the presence of pelargonidin-3-galactoside. Approximately 10-8% tannin and glucoside fragarinin are found in these strawberry rhizomes.

Strawberry seeds contain about 15% fixed oil by weight. The strawberry fruit is rich in vitamin C.

In every 100 grams of strawberry fruit, the following substances are present:

Water: 89.9 grams.

Fat: 0.50 grams.

Carbohydrates: 8.4 grams.

Calcium: 21 milligrams.

Phosphorus: 21 milligrams.

Potassium: 164 milligrams.

Vitamin A: 60 international units.

Vitamin C: 59 milligrams.

Additionally, it contains approximately 1% free acids such as malic acid, citric acid, vinic acid, and lactic acid.

Specifications:

Strawberry is a perennial plant. Its stem acts as an aerial stem while functioning as an underground stem at the same time. In various parts of the stem, which spreads on the ground and soil, root-bearing bases are created that go into the soil. From that point onwards, the plant's origin and new independent shrub are formed, and from the same point, its cluster-like leaves grow in groups, with all the petioles connected to a single point below. The stems produce one or more white flowers. Its fruit is a compound resembling a berry, but larger, watery, and sweet or sour and sweet depending on the variety. Strawberry is propagated by sowing its seeds, which is done immediately after harvesting in a soil mixture of sand and leaf soil in the month of August. The seeds, which are lightly covered with soil, are planted in a semi-shaded area, and as soon as the leaves appear, they are transplanted at a distance of 10 centimeters in a nursery bed. These seedlings spend the winter in the nursery bed and are planted in the field at a distance of 25 centimeters in the early spring.

The second method is to plant shoots separated from the strawberry shrub for propagation. This is done in mid-summer when the shoots are separated from the mother bases. These seedlings are planted in the waiting area to develop roots and then transferred to the original location in early autumn with a distance of 30-40 centimeters. The harvest of these bases is done in the month of June of the following year. A strawberry plant should not be harvested for more than 2-3 years from a single piece, and after that, the field and soil should be renewed and prepared.

42. Sweet Lemon

Latin name:

Lemon and Sweet lime.

Scientific name:

Citrus limettioides Tanaka, from the Rutaceae family.

Medicinal forms:

Fruit & skin.

Medicinal properties and uses:

Sweet Lemon has a cool and dry nature, and its properties are mostly similar to those of sour lemon, except that it is not sour and is not harmful to the nerves. Sweet lemon fruit is beneficial for infectious fevers and jaundice, and it has a cooling effect. Due to its sweetness, it does not have the negative effects on the nerves that sour lemon has.

The peel of sweet lemon, as well as sour lemon, is useful for rubbing on the skin to treat eczema and pimples. Boiling their peels is also beneficial for soothing coughs and relieving indigestion.

Composition:

The peel of lemon contains essential oils such as d-limonene, linalool, linalyl acetate, and others, along with a bitter substance. Fresh leaves of lemon contain approximately 0.18% essential oil, mainly composed of 26.5% d-limonene, 16.4% di-allyl, limonene, 9.24% linalool, 24.38% geraniol, and finally, 19.38% linalyl acetate.

Specifications:

Sweet lemon has a thin, smooth, light yellow skin and a sweet taste. It is cultivated in southern Iran and also in India.

43. Tangerine

Other names:
Youssef Efendi.

Latin Names:
Mandarin and Tangerine.

Scientific Name:
Citrus reticulata Blanco from the Rutaceae family.[1]

Medicinal Forms:
Fruit, Blossom, Leaf & Peel.

---

1. In Iran, two types are known: one is called C. nobilis var delicisa Swingle, and the other is called "Unshiu" C. nobilis var unshiu Swingle.

Medicinal Properties and Usage:

Tangerine fruit acts as a laxative and increases sexual potency. It is a stomach tonic, astringent, and relieves flatulence, nausea, and vomiting. Its blossoms are stimulants.

Tangerine leaves, like other citrus varieties, are used for washing wounds and reducing their pain. Other properties of its peel are similar to other citrus fruits.

Composition:

Tangerine peel contains approximately 0.5% essential oil, and essential oil is also extracted from its leaves and stems (about 0.55%).

The essential oil of tangerine peel contains d-limonene, limonene terpene, carone, and linalool, of which d-limonene and d-limonene account for about 78%, but in the essential oil of leaves and stems, namely the petitgrain essential oil, only about 42% d-limonene is found. Both types of essential oil contain about 15% linalool. Sugar and amino acids are found in tangerine juice.

In every 100 grams of peeled tangerine, the following substances exist: 87 grams of water, 11.6 grams of carbon hydrates, 0.4 grams of ash, 40 milligrams of calcium, 18 milligrams of phosphorus, 0.4 milligrams of iron, 2 milligrams of sodium, 126 milligrams of potassium, vitamin A, 169–420 international units, thiamine (B1) 0.06 milligrams, riboflavin (B2) 0.02 milligrams, niacin (B3) 0.1 milligrams, and vitamin C 31 milligrams. It provides 46 calories of energy.

Specifications:

It is a small, bushy, and fruitful tree with thin, spear-shaped leaves. Its fruit is small, and its peel is orange-red. In the bami type, the peel separates from the fruit and is sweet, while in the unshiu type, the peel is thin, smooth, stuck to the fruit, and also sweet in taste. It is cultivated in both northern and southern Iran.

44. Thorny Gooseberry

Other names for gooseberry:

Frang Ozumi, Galesh, Divanguri.

Latin names:

Gooseberry, Gooseberry Europen, Gateberry.

Scientific Name:

Ribes reclinaum (from the Saxifragaceae family).

Medicinal forms:

Fruit.

Therapeutic properties and usage:

The fruit of gooseberry is a mild laxative due to the mucilage found in its seeds. It is useful for relieving constipation. Overconsumption of gooseberry fruit is harmful and can cause disorders. Gooseberry is usually consumed as a diuretic and coolant. It is often eaten raw or unripe. For the preparation of gooseberry juice, refer to the bunch-shaped gooseberry.

Composition:

Fresh plant leaves contain hydrocyanic acid. The fruit of gooseberry contains a small amount of sugar, including approximately 7% dextrose and levulose, and about 1.5% free acids such as citric acid, malic acid, and tartaric acid. Unripe fruit contains a small amount of succinic acid and various substances such as albuminoids and tannins. The seeds contain some mucilage.

Specifications:

Thorny gooseberry is a shrub with three-branched thorny stems. The stem of the shrub is gray, and its height is less than 2 meters. Its heart-shaped leaves have sharp tips, rounded bases, and long petioles. Each leaf is divided into 5-3 parts, with serrations on the edges of each part and hairy scales covering the back and front of the leaves. The flowers tend to be greenish or purplish, and the fruit is the size of a chickpea with green skin and pistachio-like pale green flesh. Propagation of this shrub is commonly done through stem cuttings. This shrub is found in North Africa, the Caucasus, and the Himalayan regions. In Iran, it is seen in the highlands of northern forests such as Nur, Kojur, and Godook, as well as in Talar Valley at an altitude of 2400 meters above sea level.

45. Watermelon

Latin name:

Water melon.

Scientific Name:

Citrullus vulgaris from the Cucurbitaceae family.[1]

Medicinal forms:

Fruit, peel, seed, root.

Therapeutic properties and method of Usage:

In terms of its nature, it is cold and wet, and in terms of its properties, they believe that it is a remedy for the acridity of bile, blood, and thirst. It is diuretic and sweetens the production of thin blood and phlegm and makes the body fresh and fresh.

In China and Japan, the fruit, skin, flesh, and juice of watermelon are used as diuretics and stomach tonics. The skin and the edible part inside are eaten to treat jaundice, diabetes, and to relieve

---

1. This section of the book is selected, compiled, and prepared from the book "Plant Knowledge Selection, Arrangement, and Preparation."

poisoning. Watermelon flesh is useful for relieving discomfort and sores in the throat and mouth.

Watermelon juice is useful for kidney problems or nephritis, and watermelon seeds soften the skin and mucus, help digestion and soften the chest.[1]

Watermelon skin ash is used to treat thrush and oral blisters. The yellow watermelon flesh is very laxative. In Indochina, watermelon root extract is used to stop bleeding after abortion. In Indonesia, watermelon mixed with vinegar and turmeric is used to relieve rheumatic pains.

In India, watermelon seed kernel is used as an anthelmintic, and the alcoholic extract and watermelon seed oil paralyzes tapeworms and roundworms in cats. Fresh watermelon is useful for treating beriberi and relieving bladder inflammation.

Drinking watermelon juice with saffron is useful for jaundice and burnt bile, helping digestion, increasing urine secretion, and crushing kidney stones. If eaten with sugar, it is effective for cooling the body.

---

1. This type of watermelon is abundant in China.

Components:

Watermelon contains a substance called citrulline. It contains carotene, lycopene, and mannitol.[1] Watermelon seeds contain 2040% fixed oil. The fruit is weak in terms of vitamin C and provitamin A but rich in pectin. In addition, its seeds are a rich source of urea enzyme.

Watermelon juice contains about 0.17% citrulline. Its seed oil acts as a substitute for almond oil. Another study shows that watermelon contains a type of sugar that has diuretic effects. It also contains a type of salt that treats kidney swelling and inflammation. Multiple experiments have shown that the substance cocurbitin, which is present in watermelon, is beneficial for reducing and treating high blood pressure or hypertension. Studies conducted in India have shown that glutamic acid, derived from the residue of watermelon, has positive effects on brain functions.

Watermelon seeds, when their oil is extracted, are effective in treating cognitive and intellectual deficiencies in children and adolescents.

In every 100 grams of edible watermelon, the following substances are present: 92 grams of water, 5 grams of protein, 0.2 grams of fat, 6.1 grams of carbohydrates, 7 milligrams of

---

1. Mannitol is a type of sugar alcohol. It is a white crystalline substance with the formula (HOCH2CHOH) CH2OH. This substance is also found in the manna obtained from the flower of the tamarisk tree. Mannose, a hexose sugar with the raw formula C6H12O6, is also derived from the hydrolysis of mannans. Mannitol is one of the sugars that is not completely absorbed by the body.

calcium, 10 milligrams of phosphorus, 0.5 milligrams of iron, 1 milligram of sodium, 100 milligrams of potassium, 590 IU of vitamin A, 0.03 milligrams of thiamine, 0.03 milligrams of riboflavin, 0.2 milligrams of niacin, and 75 milligrams of vitamin C.[1]

Specifications:

Watermelon is a one-year-old plant closely related to melons. Its stem is branched and has a hairy, creeping, and angular stalk with wide alternating leaves that divide into five parts, each with serrations on the edges.

Its flowers are small and yellow. The fruit is round or elongated, large, with smooth and glossy skin, often green but sometimes pale green or marbled. After ripening, the flesh inside turns red, and the seeds and rind of the fruit vary in color, including black, white, red, or yellow.

It is native to Africa and grown in most parts of the world. Different indigenous varieties of watermelon are grown in most regions of Iran.

---

[1]. Another report states that a new amino acid called alpha-beta (pyrazolylane) propionic acid has been isolated from watermelon fruit, and beta-pyrazol-8-ylalanine, an amino acid, has been identified in its seeds.

46. White Mulberry[1]

Other names:
Toos Farsad, Dot, Taki (fruit).

Latin name:
White mulberry.

Scientific name:
Morus Alba L.

Family:
Moraceae.

---

1. White mulberry has a variety that has a dark liver color. Its scientific name is Morus alba var nigra, and it is also called black mulberry. Note that this is not the same as the king mulberry; black mulberry has the same taste and properties as white mulberry, but only the color of its fruit is black. The best type of white mulberry root bark is clean, white, and flexible. There are two common methods for preparing the root bark before consumption in China: The first method involves washing and soaking the dried root bark in water until it becomes soft, then cutting it into small pieces and stir-frying it. The second method involves taking 50 kilograms of dried root bark, mixing it with boiling water and 15 kilograms of honey, and simmering it gently until the barks turn yellow. Then they are taken out, flattened, and dried.

Medicinal forms:

Fruit, leaves, twigs, bark & roots.

Therapeutic properties and usage

White mulberry, also known as sweet mulberry or simply sweet fruit, is warm and moist in nature. Its properties include blood-building, refreshing the brain, and relieving congestion. It is beneficial for the liver and aids in weight gain. It is also useful for enhancing sexual potency, diuretic, and having a laxative effect. It is beneficial for measles and rashes. However, according to Avicenna, despite all these benefits, it spoils the blood and causes headaches and gastric disturbances in individuals with cold temperament. Therefore, individuals with cold temperament should consume it with sour sumac.

In China, the bark, roots, young twigs, leaves, and fruits of white mulberry are used in traditional medicine.

The roots are extracted from the soil in winter, thoroughly washed and cleaned, longitudinally incised, and then the skin separates easily. They are then packaged and dried in the sun.

White mulberry root bark is cool and refreshing, and it is used for treating various respiratory diseases. It is also used for continuous thirst, especially for treating high blood pressure and numbness in hands and feet. The juice of young twigs and leaves is also used for relieving numbness in hands and feet. Mulberry leaves, when harvested after frost in the months of December &

January, have better effects. They are harvested, packaged, and dried. In summer, some young twigs and leaves are also harvested and stored. After eating mulberry leaves, they taste bitter and sweet. They have a cooling and fever-reducing effect, cool the blood, reduce inflammation, make the eyes bright, and are recommended for colds, severe coughs, redness and inflammation of the eyes.

Infusions of mulberry leaves are useful for reducing eye swelling. Additionally, drinking infusions of mulberry leaves and young twigs cleanses the blood and promotes blood production.

White mulberry fruit is consumed for all the purposes for which the root bark is used, along with its properties as an antidote. It is also used for treating rheumatism. Young twigs, young fruit stems, and root bark of mulberry, all have strengthening, invigorating, diuretic properties. They are useful for softening the chest, relieving coughs, asthma, chest diseases, edema, rheumatism, and purging. The leaves are blood-purifying, cooling, and digestive. The fruit relieves thirst and provides strength by promoting blood production.

Components:

The skin of white mulberry root contains beta-sitosterol, resinotannol, and a small amount of essential oil. The leaves contain carotene, succinic acid, adenine, choline, amylase, and the eggs contain urease. The fruit contains vitamin C, carbohydrates, and citric acid. The plant's ash contains a significant amount of calcium carbonate and salicylic acid.

Specifications:

The bark of the tree reaches a height of 3 to 4 meters and a diameter of up to one meter. The bark is grooved and grayish-yellow. The leaves vary, with some having smooth and palmate margins, while others have dentate margins. The color of the leaves is bright green and shiny, with a long petiole.[1] The fruit is compound, cylindrical, with a peduncle. The length of the fruit varies from 2 to 4 centimeters, and its color can be white, sugary, or even liver-colored, depending on the different types. It is sweet in taste.

---

1. White Mulberry leaves are used in spring for sericulture (silkworm cultivation), and they are used for feeding silkworms. In autumn, they are used as animal feed. The wood of the tree is widely used in carpentry, such as for making threads.

47. Wild Tomato (Solanum pimpinellifolium)

Other names:

Ajaseh, Bari Haleh (Halaneh), Khaledar.

Latin name:

Sloe tree or Blackthorn.

Scientific name:

Prunus spinosa, and it belongs to the Rosaceae family.

Medicinal properties and usage:

In terms of nature, it is cool and moist like a sour plum, but it is cooler than sour plum, and its lint is less temperate. In some cases and for certain temperaments, it is constipating and laxative, although it is constipating for stomachs that are not clean, which is usually the case, it acts as a laxative. To alleviate the harm of sour tomatoes for cold stomachs, they are boiled and prepared with sugar or honey, which eliminates the harm in this case.

Cooked wild tomatoes in rose water have an astringent effect, and the gum of the tomato, called "Persian gum" in Persian, is warmer than Arabic gum and has less viscosity than Arabic gum. It breaks down bladder stones and is beneficial for coughing. Rubbing it on the eyes is beneficial for improving vision, and a dressing of Persian gum with vinegar is beneficial for treating children's body rashes. Boiling 40 grams of wild tomato peel in 1000 grams of astringent water is beneficial for blood formation. Boiling the peel of the stem or the root of the wild tomato in 1000 grams of water, which is consumed in 2-3 small cups, is blood-forming and laxative, and it is beneficial for cases of muscle cramps, cough, kidney stones, and reducing female secretions.

Boiling 30 grams of the fruit in 1000 grams of water is beneficial for treating bloody diarrhea. Externally, gargling with it is beneficial for reducing swelling and relieving sore throat, and if sniffed through the nose, it is beneficial for stopping nosebleeds.

Composition:

The bark of the wild tomato tree contains about 3% tannin. Its flowers contain a small amount of hydrocyanic acid (HCN) and catechin (5). In its fruit, namely the sour tomato, tannin, various malic acids, and sugars are present. Its seed contains a fatty substance and amygdalin, and from its kernel, hydrocyanic acid (HCN) is obtained.

Description:

The wild tomato shrub is short, about 1-2 meters in height, and has multiple branches with abundant leaves. Its leaves are small, ovate, with sharp or curved tips, and the edges of the leaves are serrated and curved. The fresh leaves may have some cracks, and the undersides of the leaves are smooth or slightly hairy. The dimensions of the leaves are 2.5 to 5 centimeters, and smaller. The leafstalk is smooth or hairy and is one centimeter long. Its flowers are white, early, usually solitary, rarely in pairs, and have a diameter of 1.5 centimeters. They appear in spring before the leaves, and the flower stalk is smooth or hairy, about 1 centimeter long. The fruit is round and dark blue, tending towards black, dusty, and about 1.5-2 centimeters in diameter. Its pit is egg-shaped and adheres to the flesh of the fruit, and the taste of the fruit is very sour.

The wild tomato shrub grows in Iran, Europe, Asia Minor, and the Caucasus. In Iran, it is distributed in Mazandaran, Chalous, Gilan, Nowshahr, Talesh, Manjil, Ardabil, and Arasbaran. It reproduces easily through the planting of its cuttings.

www.ingramcontent.com/pod-product-compliance
Lightning Source LLC
Chambersburg PA
CBHW071232080526
44587CB00013BA/1587